THE
ACADEMIC
TRIBES

BY HAZARD ADAMS

Nonfiction

The Academic Tribes

Fiction

The Horses of Instruction
The Truth about Dragons: An Anti-Romance

Criticism

Blake and Yeats: The Contrary Vision
William Blake: A Reading of the Shorter Poems
The Contexts of Poetry
The Interests of Criticism
Lady Gregory
Philosophy of the Literary Symbolic
Joyce Cary's Trilogies: Pursuit of the Particular Real

EDITED BY HAZARD ADAMS

Poems by Robert Simeon Adams
Poetry: An Introductory Anthology
Fiction as Process (with Carl Hartman)
William Blake: Jerusalem, Selected Poetry and Prose
Critical Theory since Plato
Critical Theory since 1965 (with Leroy Searle)

THE ACADEMIC TRIBES

SECOND EDITION

Hazard Adams

University of Illinois Press
Urbana and Chicago

Chapter 1 appeared originally in *The American Scholar.*

Selection from Chapter 8 reprinted by permission of *The New Republic,* © 1974, *The New Republic, Inc.*

Excerpts from W. H. Auden's "Under Which Lyre," copyright © 1946. From *W. H. Auden: Collected Poems,* edited by Edward Mendelson. Reprinted by permission of Random House, Inc.

A section of Chapter 2 on humanistic study appeared originally in the *Irvine Humanities Review.*

The triptych of appendixes appeared originally in the *ADE Bulletin.* They are reprinted here by permission of the Association of Departments of English.

Library of Congress Cataloging-in-Publication Data

Adams, Hazard, 1926–
    The academic tribes.

    1. Universities and colleges—United States—
Administration.   2. College teachers—United States.
I. Title.
LB2341.A3   1988   378.73   87-19051
ISBN 0-252-01441-3 (cloth: alk. paper)
ISBN 0-252-06000-8 (paper: alk. paper)

CONTENTS

PREFACE TO
THE SECOND EDITION

TWELVE YEARS HAVE PASSED since this book was first published. It would be, I think, a mistake to attempt minor revisions. Thus, I have let the text stand exactly as it was in 1976, with regret for anachronisms like "women's libbers" (since happily replaced by "feminists") and for the somewhat dated types described in chapter 6. My principles and antinomies, however, seem to me to stand up fairly well, and the impulse in years intervening between 1976 and the present has been but to add to them. A few additions may be found in the triptych of appendixes that has been added to this new edition. One further principle not mentioned in them I offer in the form of a warning to administrators contemplating return to full-time teaching: *The returned administrator becomes a COMMITTEE-PERSON.* The three essays of the triptych first appeared in the *ADE Bulletin* of the Association of Departments of English in the years 1977, 1983, and 1985; the second one was reprinted in *Profession 83*. All were originally presented as addresses at meetings of the Association, and I am grateful to it for permission to reprint them here with a few slight revisions.

The last decade has not been a good one for higher education. Long ago A. N. Whitehead observed that when one looked at the state of education one could barely suppress a savage rage. He was speaking, as I recall, of the institution of education in itself. For the most part this book deals with higher education internally and, where possible, tries to substitute irony for rage. However, it would be more difficult to do this today, for such a book would have to deal at some length with the forces working from the outside on higher education—the electorate, the politicians, the Department of Education, and the technological complex. The appendixes touch on some of the problems that humanists, particulary English departments, have had and are having under the conditions recently prevailing, but they do not discuss the relation of the tribes named above to higher education. I am not sure that the parody of anthropological analysis would any longer serve if I were to take on that onerous and depressing task. Perhaps contemporary analyses of power along Foucauldian lines could provide a model, or a parody of criminology.

PREFACE TO
THE FIRST EDITION

THIS IS A BOOK about academic life and politics, in which I induce certain principles of tribal behavior on the basis of personal and quite unscientific observation. When the first chapter was published separately in *The American Scholar* in 1973, I was horrified to receive a request to include it in an anthology of scholarly papers on education. I declare here and now that I have read as little scholarship in the fields of educational and organizational theory as is conceivable, given my academic experience. My book makes no claims to any kind of abstract knowledge in these subjects. Indeed, I proceed with a skepticism about them that I hope only gradually sinks into ill temper. For the most part, I intend my chapters to be good-natured musings that have arisen out of personal experience—as an administrator, but always as a teacher. I like to think that, while I was administering, continued teaching helped me to maintain perspective; but that is finally for others to judge. My experience in recent years has been in state universities, and this is reflected in what I have to say, though I am sure someone with experience principally in a private institution will be able to transpose. In any case, I make no claims to universal wisdom.

My main debt is to Oscar Wilde, whose spirit I like to

think would brood with approval over Chapter 6. I doubt that Immanuel Kant would regard the antinomies induced in Chapter 1 as possessing philosophic rigor, and I therefore do not embarrass his spirit, if it broods, with thanks.

A further note: throughout this book I have used the pronoun "he" rather than endlessly repeating the awkward "he or she" or the deadening "person." Please know, however, that "he" refers to both men and women. It might have been hoped, incidentally, that the recent appearance of women in somewhat greater numbers on faculties would have wrought the possibility of changes in the principles I induce and of reduction in the barbarism of some rituals. I sadly see no evidence of this to date. Even such a hope may be regarded as chauvinistic, for all I know.

Newport Beach, California   HAZARD ADAMS
November 1975

. . . Thou shalt not sit
With statisticians nor commit
A social science.
—W. H. AUDEN

THE
ACADEMIC
TRIBES

Chapter 1

A PRIMER OF
ACADEMIC POLITICS

NOT LONG AGO, before I left academic administration, I had a conversation at a leisurely evening party with a lawyer who lectured part time at a state university. He was a friendly fellow intent on feeling me out, so he turned the conversation to the problems of administering such a university. Interspersed among his questions were occasional protests against the shockingly small amount of time that he claimed it took law professors to discharge their academic duties. Like many other people these days, he thought something should be done about "this sort of thing," and he suggested that the era of the "academic administrator" ought perhaps to come to an end and that the new administrator would have to be someone specifically trained in administration as such, or someone with the requisite experience from business—that is, practical real life. By all this he seemed to mean what I take many current speakers before conventions of university administrators to mean: the new administrator must be conversant with the law, the niceties of labor arbitration, systems analysis, and sophisticated budgeting methods. Above all, he must be sensitive to the requirement that academic institutions be *accountable*. Accountable for *what* or to *whom* is, of course, the real question. And that raises the further question of politics, a subject of special weirdness when it is limited to academic politics.

Being a professor in the liberal arts and sciences mold who passed up through the administrative ranks, so to speak, I blanched inwardly at my friend's vision of some marvelous, perfectly prepared, and wholly competent administrator who was going to render me obsolete as surely as the auto replaced the horse or the T formation the single wing. My response was the response of so many practically experienced people who have scoffed, sometimes in fear, at the theoretically trained newcomer. It was the response of the warrant officer to the shavetail, the general practitioner to the specially trained new intern. I found myself suddenly on the side of practical experience after a substantial academic career that had been devoted naturally to the manifest virtues of contemplation and theory. It was an extremely uncomfortable position.

—Until it occurred to me that my training and experience ought to have made me adept at the strategies of argumentation, even in conversation with lawyers. At once I maneuvered to shift the ground of the argument itself. I declared that my friend's proposal was based on a false analogy. He assumed that universities were businesses or some mode of civil service. It was all very well, I said, for people to be appropriately trained for their jobs, but the model he had in mind was wrong. Universities were more like political organizations, microcosmic nations of a very special sort. The model had originally been monastic, but with respect to the universities' political life that model had been abandoned long ago. The appropriate training would have to be a special political training. Since no one had ever managed to determine what political training ought to be like, I felt that I could rest easy in my practical experience. I knew my friend could argue that there *should* be specific political training for my sort of job, along with the development of certain special skills. My friend, however, was polite, showing the deference that the community gives to academics when they are met socially in groups of not more than one.* Had he pursued the argument, I could have conjured up the frightening image of tyranny exploited by experts in governing. If there is the incompetence of disorganization, there is also the tyranny of planners.

Thus, secure in my own dogma that there ought to be a certain amount of profanity in any political perfection, and having declared that universities are political in nature, I had justified my existence to myself. Furthermore, there tramped through my mind as I argued a herd of recent incidents in which I had found it necessary in my administrative role to cope with the various naïvetés and exuberances of the model-building or planning intellect. Finally, my friend retreated from argument, leaving me with an opportunity that no true professor contemplating an empty lectern can resist: I delivered myself of the usual fifty minutes. The informally schematic notes that follow are a reconstruction thereof.

I

I begin with the six Principles of Faculty-Administration Polity. These Principles are to be followed in this chapter by the two Antinomies of Pure Administration, which with the Principles mark the boundaries and ironies of academic behavior. Admittedly, all of this smacks of the model-building intellect itself, but my designing of Principles and Antinomies is better regarded as a ritual acceptance of the total irony implied by all, taken together. I must add that I firmly believe that the Principles apply to the *best* of all possible academic situations; thus they have a somewhat idealistic tinge, and many professors in institutions where the policies are depressingly cruder and various safeguards are absent will not

* Under these conditions each side treats the other as an emissary of a foreign culture and behaves with restraint.

recognize them as describing an actuality of their lives. I warn other readers against dismissing them as an expression of cynicism or as an excuse for radical reform. They are meant simply to offer a classic vision of what one had better contract for in the face of far less appealing alternatives.*

After inducing the Principles and Antinomies I shall present some informal sociological remarks on the various "Estates" of the university: students, nonfaculty employees, the external community, faculty, and administration. These are offered by way of introduction to the chapters that follow.

Principle the First: The Diffusion of Academic Authority. This Principle states that *no one has the complete power to do any given thing.* It describes a condition which is old and revered and about which there is nevertheless bitter complaint without the plaintiff's knowing quite where to direct it. In the sixties, rebellious students, considering themselves the oppressed majority, sought the oppressor in the form of dean or president—the apparent colonial administrator—only to be told wistfully that he was powerless to perform magical acts of emancipation or even to effect "significant change." Faculty members, too, often succumb to frustration and accuse administrators of passing the buck or sending them and their ideas in a huge bureaucratic circle. The community is horrified at the president's "unwillingness" to discipline dissidents.

The fact is that real authority in the university is not hierarchical, as in business or the military; it is not even "separate" as it is in principle in the United States government. There is not a system of checks and balances so much as a

---

* This view is borne out by the fact that some faculties that do not enjoy much power have entered into collective bargaining in order to bring about a situation in their institutions more nearly approximating what the Principles imply as ideal.

diffusion of authority. According to academic mythological history, there was once a pleasant Eden where the university was truly collegial and all administrative chores came about as a result of a division of responsibilities among faculty members. Minimal administration was a necessary housekeeping task, and professors were their own bosses and professed their subjects, answerable only to their disciplines. Modern life does not tolerate this Edenic simplicity, and human nature deplores a power vacuum.* Yet the myth persists of this Golden Age before the dissociation of academic sensibility set in, presumably in America around the time of the Land Grant Act. It was then that the modern administrator appeared, perhaps from the sea or from the rocks and caves of crass commercialism. In fact, the administrator emerged from the faculty itself. With the advent of public higher education, universities became the taxpayers' business, and the administrator was soon no longer a housekeeper but a Mr. Facing-both-ways. Fact or fiction, from this disaster, it is said, we have never recovered.

Vestiges of the Golden Age remain. In the best of all possible fallen institutions, the faculty controls courses, curriculum, academic requirements, and the like. The administration controls the budget. Personnel matters exist in the shady area in between. It is not really separation, but diffusion of powers. The administration has no formal veto power over curriculum and no power to institute it; however, the faculty has no power to finance curriculum, while the administration, if it chooses, can destroy a curriculum by withholding or decreasing budget. It can also hold out the carrot of funding for a new program to an otherwise mulish faculty. (Principle

* One of the ironic situations we observed over the last several years was the surfacing of a belief among some students and some faculty members that this Edenic situation could be restored almost instantly and *not* by divine intervention. Many administrators know that some of the faculty like to regard administrative jobs as still having this Edenic simplicity: administrators merely shuffle paper, et cetera, et cetera.

the Second will explain to us why administrators rarely do the former.) On matters of promotion and appointment to its ranks the faculty only recommends, with the final decision the administrator's; but in fact faculty power is certainly as great as, if not greater than, the administrator's in this matter, since only the faculty originates recommendations, and an administrator rarely is successful in persuading a faculty to originate a proposal that he desires (as Principle the Fourth will explain). Further, an administrator is in trouble (see several later Principles) if he acts more than once in a blue moon contrary to faculty personnel recommendations. Even one such move becomes of disproportionate importance, driving everyone to standing on principle. When an administrator does act contrary to advice, he may choose to plead budgetary necessity in order to sanctify his decision. But administrators are not sacred in the least and must remember this, whether response to them is sycophantic or cacophonous.

In those new-style multicampus institutions that have sprung up in some of the more populous states, diffusion spreads not only from the campus administrator to the faculty but also in the direction of the system's central bureaucracy. It has been said that the least powerful person in such institutions is the president or chancellor (depending on nomenclature) and that the best he can do is keep reasonably abreast of what is going on in his diffuse organization. This is necessary so that he can devote himself to inventing answers to legislative complaint, a full-time job leaving little time for decisions. No matter, the argument continues, since his decisions could rarely be enforced.

The upshot of Principle the First is that the administrator's role is political rather than executive, that his direct authority is limited and usable only rarely, and that his indirect powers of persuasion are useful if sufficient support in the faculty can be rallied and if he is able to maintain his position as a Necessary Symbol (Principle the Sixth). I claim that this is the best of all possible situations, as meager as its potentiality appears to those who deplore its inefficiencies.

Principle the Second: The Deterioration of Academic Power. No doubt there are exceptions to this principle. Nonetheless, *real academic power deteriorates from the moment of an administrator's first act.* One reason for this is the new administrator's huge initial psychological advantage. He is at the outset a pristine, abstract symbol. Others, at lower levels, are vying for power and want to gain the initial advantage that co-operation with him will bring. More accurately, of course, they genially seek out his co-operation in *their* endeavors. But all administrators play a zero-sum game. The funding that they send in one direction goes in none of the others. To pass out largesse in some perfectly "fair" fashion is only to increase frustration all around among entrepreneurs and special interests. Since real administrative power is so often the power of persuasion, and budgetary allocation is so often determined by the situation of the moment, the administrator's persuasive power is ironically eroded by his budgetary authority, such as it is: the imperatives of allocating budget often raise the hackles of those he wishes to persuade.

Another kind of administrative power is also subject to deterioration. That is the power to act affirmatively in response to ideas arising from the faculty. Here, too, the administrator is often in the position of having to go to the faculty as a whole to seek what only a portion of the faculty desires. Thus every act diminishes somewhere the good will with which the administrator begins. With each act he descends into politics. Of course, in his interplay with faculty, students, regents, and the community, these groups lose their symbolic purity as well.

The administrator at any level—whether chairman, dean, or president—suffers a worm's-eye view of human nature, even as the faculty observes each administrator abandon one by one the faculty's cherished principles. The administrator learns that faculty members on occasion must be bailed out of jail; helped through nervous collapses; suffered to insult the surrounding community, including possible donors of gifts; expected to corrupt the lives of students—to seduce, rape, or even marry them; and tolerated in their unauthorized use of the phones, the mail, and the university's name. In other words, with respect to these matters they are no different from anyone else.

The faculty member, on the other hand, observes the administrator co-operate with people he believes are insidious fools at best and, apparently taken in by them, opt for the clearly pragmatic solution. In such situations—again I see no escaping them—the faculty observes the symbol of the institution tarnished even as it reveals its human dimensions, while the administrator is tempted toward misanthropy as he copes endlessly with problems of personality and character in a faculty proudly exercising its independence.

It would appear that any administrator should gauge his effectiveness and plan to step out of office and into faculty ranks in due time. That he have a place there to go to is important. In order to maintain it, he must preserve his professorial qualifications and not become estranged from his subject by losing touch with the scholarship in his field. Of course, administrators often move upward or laterally from institution to institution. Those who do this are perhaps exhibiting their capacity to anticipate the worn-out welcome.

Principle the Third: The Diminishment of Organizational Allegiance. The third Principle states that *the fundamental allegiance of the faculty member will be to the smallest unit to which he belongs.* This is usually the department, but it may not be, for two reasons. First, departments themselves have become so large in certain disciplines that they have created subdivisions. Second, some departments divide up into research groups that become very close-knit and compete with each other for support. In any case, allegiance will be to the smallest group, and administrators must count on this as a political fact. Faculty members suddenly thrust into responsibility for a course or program that crosses over such units or draws from a variety of them know this Principle well and come to resent it vehemently because it frustrates the success of the more informally constructed units that they are attempting to build. By the same token, interdepartmental programs often press to become departments themselves, if the original allegiances are successfully submerged by the new venture.

Obviously, this Principle has unfortunate consequences. There is, as a result, much complaint in academe against departmentalization. Some campuses have experimented with large departmentless schools or colleges. Two problems may arise when this is tried. First, the individual faculty member may turn inward toward the one manageable unit he recognizes—in this situation, himself—and come to regard himself as a freewheeling entrepreneur answering only vaguely to some distant dean. Or he may be engulfed in a highly centralized organization manipulated by a dean with no checks against the dean's will, disorganization being a ready excuse for unilateral administrative action.

Some campuses have tried to compromise by creating two interlocking structures—a residential college, to which each faculty member belongs, and a department or board of study, to which each faculty member also belongs. Both organizations develop curricula, and both make demands on faculty time, by doubling committee work, which the faculty generally detests anyway, and by increasing the institution's political complexity.

Principle the Third asserts that a faculty member is inevitably tugged in a certain direction opposite to that of the administration. Deans and presidents are, therefore, often viewed as representing an alien interest. Administrators tend to view faculty as intransigent or disorganized because of this. They are best advised to represent themselves to the faculty quite clearly as responsible for the total intellectual and educational enterprise of the institution; else they will surely be regarded simply as the enemy that constantly chooses crass expediency. It is important politically, if for no other reason, to articulate an intellectual position upon which to base administrative actions in behalf of the whole. It will be in behalf of the more parochial but deeply felt interests of the smallest units that these actions will be opposed. Faced with rational appeals for unity, faculties will be more likely to meet such acts with respect, although probably with only slightly less opposition. The ensuing arguments will be at least better mannered. At the same time, a few faculty will usually agree with any administrative position and even support it at the expense of departmental autonomy. Sometimes, these are the people the administrator would be just as happy to have against him.

Universities have become so large and diverse that articulation of intellectual positions in their behalf is often thought to be impossible. It is more likely, however, that administrators become so embroiled in matters of immediate concern that thoughtful statements of this sort simply are never quite uttered. This problem for administrators is connected to the next Principle.

In view of the ubiquity of Principle the Third, administrators and faculty might well examine the organization of their institution to see whether a more even balance between allegiance to the whole and to the part might be achieved. It would be a neat trick to improve the situation, but until it is turned, Principle the Third applies.

Principle the Fourth: The Luxury of Principle; or, The Third Law of Academic Motion. Simply put, this Principle asserts that *to every administrative action there is an equal and opposite reaction.*

In every faculty there is a large number of people who take seriously the necessity of debating the matter of ethical principle beneath every act. This is natural, commendable, and necessary if the institution is to remain open to thought. Still, the philosopher who insisted that one should beware the man who always stands on principle said something worth remembering.

In a group of intellectuals as diverse as a university faculty, virtually any position, and particularly one espoused by the administration, will generate a reaction founded on principle. A simple, perhaps depressing, generalization: the administration that takes a clear line on an educational issue will be countered by those who argue that an administration should limit itself to carrying out faculty policy, while the administration that awaits faculty action will be declared, in time, to be indecisive and without principle. In any case, at every level, an administration can expect accusations of unprincipled behavior in equal reaction to action. This cannot be avoided, for several reasons. There are always a few people in the faculty who will regard any single issue as a problem to be worked out simply for the sake of the adventure involved. Faculties are, after all, composed largely of people who like problems, perhaps even more than solutions, and even to the point of actively seeking them where they have not been recognized. Indeed, some of these individuals positively dislike solutions, preferring the deeper existential absurdity of the problem itself.

Also, there is the "Oedipal" element in the relation of faculty to administration, which I conveniently wrench from its Freudian meaning to use as a catchword for a variety of rebellious motives. On the administrative side there is the "Creon complex," which I employ to stand for a tendency of administrators to abstract from a mass of individual negative reactions the image of general bovine resistance to reason. Most administrators know that faculty and administration alike

react to one another more negatively in the late months of the
academic year, when patience is frayed. Therefore, a corollary to Principle the Fourth is that nothing should be done in
May that can be put off to October.

Related to the Oedipal element is the protective reaction
that a faculty will evince against an administrative decree
while at the same time breathing a sigh of relief at its is-
suance. This occurs occasionally with respect to such matters
as the police, dogs, obscenity, and the like. These thoughts
lead to consideration of the next Principle, which also involves the matter of self-protection.

*Principle the Fifth: The Protective Coloration of Eccentricity. Ec-
centricity is not only to be tolerated in academic life, it is often a positive virtue.* This Principle in one of its myriad examples was
first reported by Mary McCarthy in her monograph *The
Groves of Academe.* She gives attention to the obnoxious and incompetent faculty member who so identifies himself with
radical politics that it becomes impossible to dismiss him
without appearing to have done so for political reasons. In
academic politics this game has frequently been played, but it
is merely a variation on the Principle, which also includes a
curious twist on the Peter Principle.* For example, one professor whom I know, a talented poet and teacher, was finally
beseeched by his chairman to absent himself from campus
during the advising and registration period because his advice
to students in bureaucratic matters was, though imaginative,
inevitably disastrous and time-wasting to all involved in the
registration process. He followed the chairman's advice, to

---

* The Peter Principle, developed by Professor Laurence J. Peter, asserts
that everyone rises to his level of incompetence. The exception to this rule is
the person who cleverly feigns incompetence at a lower level in order to escape the ultimate fate. The exception is our concern here. (It is not the exception cited by C. Northcote Parkinson, where incompetence is feigned *in order*
to gain control of a moribund organization.)

everyone's relief. One imagines that in order to prolong his vacation annually this crafty poet may have acted by design. His conduct was, in any case, accepted as having a sort of metaphysical fitness since, after all, poets *are* that way. Few people bothered to notice that another poet headed the department's advising program.

My Principle states that eccentricity is not merely tolerated, it is positively admired. The model for the researcher is the genius. Genius is eccentric. Therefore researchers should be eccentric. The model of political acceptability is thus very nearly turned on its head by academe. Graduates recall eccentricities among their professors with bemused nostalgia. Occasionally someone will view an apparent diminishment of eccentricity among his colleagues with alarm. It is declared to be an unnatural, dispiriting trend.

With this force of sentiment behind it, eccentricity is a defense against being drawn into committee work or a means of gaining a student following. It is often, in this case, a form of Oedipal revolt, and as such nicely illustrates Principle the Fourth.

At the same time, the administrator will often be judged negatively unless he sheds what eccentricity he had as a faculty member, or it turns miraculously into an acceptable charisma. Eccentricity is a symbol of the scholar's intellectual freedom, to say nothing of his stubbornness. The tolerance of eccentricity, although sometimes puzzling to outsiders, is inevitable in academic life, despite the range of irresponsibility it sometimes protects.

Principle the Sixth: The Necessity of Symbolism. While faculty members generally prize eccentricity and speak nostalgically of well-known eccentrics in the mythological history of their institutions, their intellectual predilections are toward abstract models of all experience and behavior. As a result, while they will defend eccentricity to the limit and eschew various forms of conventional appearance themselves, *faculties demand the proper maintenance of the symbols of their institutions.* Within the university there is a scale of symbolic conventions of behavior and appearance reaching from the pure variable of the anthropologists (itself a convention of uniqueness), through the constant search for the fashionable radical style among certain social scientists, all the way across center to that badge of authority, the medical white jacket. A sociology of appearance and behavior obviously needs to be written, to give adequate attention to the many grades on this scale and to the existential projections from various professional schools into the conventions of the community at large.

Most necessary, however, is the functioning of the president, and perhaps the dean, as symbol of the whole institution. As long as the president is subject to Principle the First, it is important to the faculty—a matter of protection—that he *seem* to exercise authority. Also, if he did not, Principle the Fourth, involving Oedipal reaction, would be no fun for anyone, and a valuable tension would relax into flabby elasticity.

The president must therefore be a role player, a supreme actor, judged as such by many faculty members, including some of those who are professional critics. Since often there is no script, the performance is of the *commedia dell' arte* type. The faculty does not hesitate to discuss the matter of "how he was today." The president must be capable of being regarded as somewhat *different* or aloof; yet on occasion he must be able to descend from his Olympian heights to demonstrate charmingly what was always really known—that he's a good guy after all. This may be accomplished in a variety of ways, including playing the clarinet, tossing the caber, or occasionally irritating the governor on television. It is always less effective when a political end is in mind, however. To accept a pie in the face at the spring carnival is, therefore, to go too far.

Some presidents, I am told, have adopted a continuous

good-guy, jeans-and-hip-jargon symbolism. Where this occurs, one can expect anxious searches for substitute symbols
of respect/resistance, and at least minor calamities.* Although
I have not myself experienced such a situation, I regard it as
intolerable, since it represents the president's own Oedipal
rejection of the Principles, and must be considered insincere.
Such behavior should be delegated to the dean of students, if
it must occur.

II

Now, as I promised, I follow the Principles with the two Antinomies pertaining to administration's relations with faculty.

*Antinomy the First: The faculty is the university; the faculty are
employees of the university.* This Antinomy was first publicly uttered at Columbia University while Dwight Eisenhower was
its president. Unfortunately, only the latter half was uttered
by Eisenhower; the first half was uttered by a faculty member. Both were right, both wrong, and the double utterance
created an adversary relationship. That the faculty is the university is an idea hearkening back to the Golden Age before
the Fall. That the faculty are employees reflects the post-
Edenic condition of public education and the growing call for
accountability of public institutions to the people. I submit
that neither concept alone is sufficient, either purity a disaster.

The public should recognize that for the faculty to declare
itself to be the university is not necessarily an arrogance. It
can be a commitment to the intellectual disciplines the faculty
professes, the end appropriately being the preservation in a
state of development of those disciplines for the sake of the

---

* My position can be described as Heraclitean. It was Heraclitus who said
Homer was mistaken when he prayed for the disappearance of strife from the
universe. He did not know he was praying for its destruction.

culture in general. Students understood this idea in a rudimentary way when they expressed outrage at university involvement in war research, which they regarded as inhuman and against any sensible cultural aims. Major universities seen as faculties are both teaching and research organizations, inasmuch as research is a form of teaching in the larger sense and both are done in behalf of culture.

But the other view is equally true. Faculty are paid, and they gain the benefits that accrue to employees of large organizations. People paid are responsible to the people who pay, even though it is recognized by those who pay that in this case the relationship is a special one and that only limited control and interference is tolerable. This is the reason that the people set up a special body with its own constitutional independence to mediate between them and the state university. By this act, the people officially acknowledge both sides of the Antinomy. Of course, some citizens do not understand this; but it is also true that some faculty do not understand it either and behave with undisguised contempt toward any public commentary or any questions at all about their activities. This is only to be expected, since all institutions are from time to time abused by individuals within them, their virtues made to appear as weaknesses by those who exploit them.

In the next few years we can expect that the latter half of the Antinomy will be in the ascendant, and much effort will have to be expended by administrations to explain the first half so that it seems at least sensible.

Antinomy the Second: The Administration is the master of the faculty; the administration is the servant of the faculty. This Antinomy is meant to summarize ideas already expressed in the Principles. I have already remarked that faculty wish and do not wish strong leadership. Their ambivalence is precisely the existential projection of this Antinomy and is an inevitable condition. Faculty and administration in their behavior recognize that *both* halves of this Antinomy together are true; each separately is false. The appearance of control and order is important. The willingness to serve is equally important. But the administrator who believes that he exists only to put into practice what the faculty proposes is likely to be in trouble, and the institution to drift. Faculty members propose conflicting things; faculties find it difficult to act in concert. The administrator must anticipate faculty desires, or make the faculty think he has, and thus serve its members' interests in one way or another.

The consequence of the Antinomy is that the administrator should have sensitivity to faculty feeling and to the idea of the disciplines that the faculty professes. This is most likely to be present in someone who has had considerable experience as a faculty member. There is no real substitute in formal training for this experience, save in the extraordinary individual. Yet it is obviously only one of the requirements for success.

III

To have cited the Principles of Faculty-Administration Polity and the Antinomies of Pure Administration at the outset is not by any means to have exhausted the fundamentals of academic politics, for the Principles and Antinomies do not deal with relationships between these groups and the other Estates, as I call them. It is clear that faculty-student and administration-student relations will engender further sets of Principles and perhaps Antinomies of equal splendor. A systematic induction of these Principles and Antinomies cannot be undertaken here. The art is not that far advanced. I leave room for further investigation; however, for the neo-Adamsians who doubtless will follow, I offer some comments that any additional categorical analysis will have to take into account (I shall report the results of further field work in subsequent chapters). Among the Estates are students, non-faculty employees, the community, and again faculty and administration.

Students. Academic politics is heavily regulated by mass student behavior, for students are the basis for budgetary allocation. Faculties and all university services are affected by how many students enroll, the attrition of enrollment through the year, how many students major in a given subject, how many choose to live on campus, and so forth. These circumstances, in turn, arise out of a complexity of many individual choices governed by social and cultural dynamics. Only in recent years has an entity known as "the students" been regarded as a force in *academic* politics. Indeed, in the usual sense students are not such a force. They are either intensely individual, seeking educational and career goals, or intensely statistical, representing budgetary units worth so many support dollars. As academic political groups, their effect is evanescent over an extended period because their aims are divergent, their stay at the university is comparatively short, and their pursuit of career interests conflicts for the most part with commitment to academic political activity. As a result, students engaged even in the politics of student government represent a special category of comparatively small size. They are involved because the activity interests them, because they belong to a specific group seeking special reforms, or in a few cases because they see student politics as offering professional training or, at least, professional advantage. On occasion, as in recent times, one can expect massive student activity, but this activity is rarely generated by the university itself or its internal workings. Instead, its sources are political or cultural forces in the larger sense. The movement toward student lobbying in the legislature, as in California, is a new development and is spawning a new bureaucracy of its own. Just whom it will eventually represent is not yet clear.

It is possible to isolate roughly three groups in the student body: first, there are the student politicians, who are heading in the direction of careers somehow vaguely connected with such activity, or who will enter the business of student lobbying after ceasing to be students themselves. Then there is the vast middle, consisting of those who move through the university hardly affecting or being affected by student government and its politics, in spite of the fact that student government controls a sizable budget, provided by student fees, over which there is often irresponsible haggling in a mad parody of whatever structure is sanctified by the student constitution. Deans of students tend to write these outrages off in the name of the education of those involved (a large expense for a few students, incidentally); faculty ignore the whole matter as much as possible; occasionally an innocent graduate student wanders into the miasma and returns stunned or outraged, ready to do moral battle to retrieve his registration fee. Finally, there are the militant disaffected, themselves forming various groups. These surface more rapidly now— the various minorities, women's libbers, homosexuals, et cetera. By no means all who could belong to these groups do, although they attempt to speak for all who could. From time to time, when they find it to their advantage, they affect the workings of student government; but it is mainly in the larger sphere of student-administration affairs that these groups express their presence. That is a topic about which much has been said, the tactics of such groups being familiar by now, and I pass on to more general considerations.

Two attitudes toward students that I shall label "fallacies" ought to be mentioned here. First, there is the fallacy of regarding the student as "consumer," with the corollary view of the university as "supermarket" (I shall take it up again in Chapter 2). One could extend the analogy to the naming of the various courses offered, with disastrous results. The idea raises images of advertising, discounts, and special two-for-

one bargains. The analogy fails to produce anything more
profound than the vision of an endless array of student
choices, with consequent overindulgence and stomach-ache.
The second fallacy is the idea that the university exists "for
the students." There is, of course, a sense in which this is
true (I am inviting the establishment of an Antinomy here);
but without very serious qualification, the proposition is mis-
leading and dangerous to everyone involved. It is too easily
assimilable to the crude form of educational romanticism that
emphasizes the unique preciousness of the student as child
and the ends of life as purely individualized gratification. One
suspects that this attitude undermines the very goals it would
profess to serve, for the student is too easily in this vision the
passive receptor, hedonist, and egoist. On the ground that
true self-realization (or some equivalent cliché) is achieved in
creative work that carries one outside selfhood, it is perhaps
best to describe the university as "for intellect and culture"
and to insist that faculty and students alike should live up to
this ideal. Although many faculty and students recognize all
this, there are segments of both that do not, for various reasons. There are the naturally egocentric and hedonistic
young, there are those faculty who wish to recapture the age
of twenty-eight, and there are those who out of political and
sociological conviction claim that "culture" is an undesirable
bourgeois concept.

That the students play less of a role in academic politics
than might be desirable for fundamental change is something
that many observers deplore and others regard as a saving
grace in an increasingly depressing situation. The picture that
I have painted in the Principles may compel some readers to
savage rage against an apparently hopeless impasse or to an
effort to resolve an apparent stalemate through student activism. An increased student role, however, would merely
generate a set of Principles declaring, for example, an even
greater diffusion of powers, and so forth. And greater student

involvement in academic politics would decrease student involvement in the intellectual life of the university, where finally the institution can offer by far its greatest gift.

Nonfaculty Employees. This large and diverse group of people is not, after all, a recognizable entity and therefore must be subdivided. First, there is the large staff of office workers. For as long as anyone can remember, these people have mainly been attracted to the university because of the comparatively less rigid, more enlightened working society that it is supposed to be; although shortly after arrival many suffer the disorientation of revised perspective. At the same time, universities have taken advantage of their so-called attractiveness and have paid at almost every level of responsibility considerably lower salaries than would be offered in business. Universities organize in ways that would horrify any businessman, but this in itself often makes university work more interesting for the worker, if the unexpected and preposterous can be regarded as diversion. The staff is totally unenfranchised and, from the political point of view, exists in serfdom. Staff members remain in a strange apartheid, often by choice as well as compulsion, the faculty seeming to many of them almost another species. Some staff members, however, develop considerable talent for faculty-keeping and herding, and become local political powers behind the scenes.

Second, from the mass of such people, there can be distinguished two subgroups whose members come closest among university employees to faculty and students and their immediate academic concerns. They are the librarians and those people involved in the general area now often referred to as "student affairs." I take up each separately.

Librarians: Of all nonfaculty employees, the librarians seem to regard themselves as the most shamelessly exploited, and they perplex those functionaries who must create tables of organization. In many institutions their attitude is justified. Often their wages and prestige have been minimal in the light of the professional training required of them and the important functions they perform. Their unrest has turned into militancy, and it has become channeled into drives to unionize, sometimes in concert with faculty, as in some activities of the American Federation of Teachers. Indeed, the A.F.T. has swelled its ranks with librarians, who sometimes have been the base for A.F.T. organizing of the faculty. The fact is that librarians inhabit a shadowy ground between faculty and staff. Many hold advanced professional degrees, and many have considerable intellectual attainment and academic competence, and feel that they should have faculty rank. Yet they usually have no voice of any kind in university policy. The joining of faculty and librarians and perhaps other staff in a single A.F.T.-style bargaining unit is viewed with suspicion by many faculty, who can see their own unique position and power in academe diluted. This is one of the reasons that the American Association of University Professors and local faculty groups have joined the organizing enterprise, as counterrevolutionary movements, so to speak.

Over the next few years academic politics will be dominated by the issues that collective bargaining raises, and many ironies will make their appearance. For example, the end of the so-called Golden Age of higher education, the shrinking of budgets, and the anticipated decline in the number of students attending college are going to create a huge excess of potential teachers and much unrest among those who actually have jobs. The latter will fear for their own positions and the system of tenure that gives them security, and they will experience loss of salary relative to the standard of living. Inevitably they will see threats to the gains that the profession has made over the last twenty years. These pressures will drive faculties more and more to organize themselves into unions. The public will deplore this situation, although the public's own representatives will have brought it about through the pressures they will have imposed on the universities. The administrators who must respond to these pressures will have to employ more ruthless methods. In some cases these acts will be accompanied by vaguely or even overtly moralistic criticism of teachers (as has been the mode of two governors of California), which will only infuriate the teachers more and drive them into an adversary position with respect to their own institution and the government. My own view is that the vindictively moralistic approach of former Governor Reagan was counterproductive and the homiletic approach of the present Governor Brown is unproductive. Mme Blavatsky said that some unfortunate people make pacts with the Devil in order to feel that they at least have *someone* on their side. Faculty members, perhaps more willingly than other professionals, will endure a considerable amount of privation if they feel that the cause of education is being championed, but in the end they will look for cohorts.

Student-Affairs Officers: Those who are concerned with student activities and services—usually supervised by a dean of students or some like administrator—exist in another shaded area. While some librarians may be even more stringently committed to an ideal of the strict intellectual life of the campus than some faculty, this doesn't seem to be the case with the student-activities people. Indeed, there is frequently an adversary relationship between faculty and these people, particularly when they do not hold faculty appointments (but often even when they do). The group includes those involved in psychological counseling and the congeries of fashions that seem eternally to surround the subject. The pressure from them is often twofold: to build up the area of student services and to enter into academic activities under the aegis of the various therapies of the moment. At one extreme, these therapies can be sharply anti-intellectual and the whole operation antithetical to dominating faculty attitudes and almost militantly adversary to the academic programs to the extent that the programs are perceived to be elitist, antiquated in techniques, excessively rigid in requirements and standards, and the like. At the other extreme, the operation co-operates with or invades academic treme, the operations co-operates with or invades academic programs to offer situations in "experimental learning." At both extremes, tension is likely to arise and to stretch into the whole fabric of the institution. Student activities and services offices are frequently regarded as octopi, money wasters, game players, harbors for anti-intellectual failed academics, et cetera; at the same time, student activities and services people often view faculty as snobbish, elitist, behind the times, and uninterested in the "whole student." Many serious-minded people in these offices are puzzled and perturbed by this situation, and many faculty members are angered by it. In between are the students, most of whom are directly affected by the student-services operation in the dormitories and dining halls and at the health center, but only a minority of whom are involved in the many other activities that it generates. It appears that in studying the relationship between faculty and this group, one is confronted by opposed types of personality equally suspicious of each other and exhibiting serious differences about educational policy. It may well be that a Principle lurks here. It would read that every act performed by the student-affairs people in behalf of students is regarded as antithetical to student interests by faculty, and vice versa.

The Community. Academic politics is not, of course, a hermetically sealed affair. Outside forces recently have loomed larger in the internal affairs of most institutions. Does an analogy with national politics allow us to think of the community under the heading "foreign affairs"? When one attends faculty meetings, one hears talk that clearly suggests the analogy. The outer world, sometimes referred to peculiarly as the "real world," is suspect; possibly it is an enemy; often it seems incapable of understanding academic language and in possession of quite different customs and values.* One imagines, after hearing enough of this, the faculty member going out into the community with attaché case and interpreter, and possibly well armed.

It is fair to say that the community does have an astonishing ignorance of the academic society, even though it is presumably the community that has sanctioned the smaller society's existence. The individuals of the community are, by and large, quite removed from the realities of the inner life of its sanctioned institutions. This state of affairs is one reason for the necessity of a buffer group such as a board of regents. The university president himself, and other members of the administration, also play this role. They are regarded on the outside as protectors of the institution, and on the inside from time to time as having sold it out. A Principle could be established here based on the idea that a faculty characteristically moves back and forth between two poles in its attitude toward community relations. In their more depressed and paranoid moods its members claim not to understand how the community—given its apparent values—would tolerate for a moment what they do. Thus they advocate a strategy of secrecy and obfuscation. In their more missionary moods, they berate the university's public-relations office for its apparent inadequacy in defining the university's role to the community. Of course, inside the faculty itself there is a tension between the view of the university in its community-service role and the view of the university as a place set aside from the community for the purpose of thought. It is unlikely

---

* To state that the nonacademic world is the real world is to imply that the academic world is unreal. Modern youth jargon, of course, refers to many things as "unreal," usually meaning that reality is very strange. The whole point of this essay is to assert that the academic world is, if you will permit a barbarism, very real.

that the community would tolerate either extreme of this opposition, and thus one sees grounds for establishing an Antinomy here. A purely service institution would abdicate its role in teaching and theoretical research. An isolated monastic institution would increase suspicion on both sides to intolerability.

The community, perhaps inevitably, has a respect/contempt attitude toward its university, which represents to it a certain expertise and the vision of an ideal of cultural achievement, while at the same time the university's isolation proves to the community the superiority of the tough "practical" values that it cherishes as its own. (Clearly we are dealing here with stereotypes. In Chapter 2, I intend to develop the art of stereotypics and by its means examine the external and internal stereotypes of the academic tribes.)

Faculty. The Principles and Antinomies seem to imply that the faculty is, in fact, a cohesive unit. It is not. University faculties, as previously suggested, value eccentricity, or at least protect it, and divide themselves up by disciplines and units of various sorts, each of which is recognizable in academic political behavior. It is generally thought that with respect to national as well as academic politics various units occupy characteristic places on a scale ranging from liberal to conservative, although academic liberalism or conservatism seems not necessarily related to national political coloring. (I shall have more to say about this in Chapter 2.)

Too, various disciplines tend to be interested at various times in specific issues of academic politics. Among physical scientists, particularly the physicists, there is considerable interest, amounting in some cases to anxiety, about how they as a group or the campus as a whole are regarded nationally. It is a matter of face and prestige. Perhaps there is pressure of this sort among these people because of the growing importance of other scientists, particularly the biologists, and a resultant shifting of the academic social hierarchy at the physicists' expense. Such concern annoys the humanists, who consider it bad style, but have their own worries brought on by the scarcity of jobs in their subjects and an increased anxiety over matters of tenure, due process, criteria for promotion, and the like. These could be regarded as obviously appropriate human concerns, but the scientists, who generally take a more hostile attitude toward anything that smacks of unionization, look askance at such humanist humanitarian preoccupations, tending to consider them blatant examples of self-interest. (I shall look further into such tribal behavior in Chapter 3.) Clearly, the characterizations I have made here are applicable only to the present and cannot rise to the level of a Principle. Currently there is a sense of embattlement among professors of some disciplines as the growth of institutions ceases and enrollments in these disciplines actually fall.

Academic politics will surely be dominated for the foreseeable future not only by professional militance and the issue of collective bargaining but also by competition for students and struggles to preserve disciplines. Much of this warfare will take place in terms of the traditional quarrel of the pure or theoretical with the applied fields. Particularly in the social sciences, an undefined and curiously unstructured area in the first place, there is a serious tension that has led to as many splinter departments and programs as has characterized the history of Protestantism. Most social scientists seem to agree that the theoreticians and the applied people simply can't get along, and that it is always a disaster to try to keep them together. In another breath it will be declared that these very differences are what prevents real progress in the field. In general it might be said that while scientists work in teams, and humanists, although usually independent scholars, have in common a certain style, social scientists, who study human group behavior to a great extent, are paradoxically the most anarchic of academic political groups. The theory-and-practice split also dominates politics in the area of the fine arts, where artists notoriously resent the assertions of critics and historians, who they often claim hate art. Where quarreling has become traditional, one is tempted to discover an Antinomy. I have claimed, however, that my Principles and Antinomies either are in the nature of things or ought to be fictively so regarded. Further, I have claimed no cynicism for them and warn future investigators against asserting the inevitability or the advisability of separating theorists and practitioners.

There is little doubt that certain habits of thought and personality go together with certain disciplines, particularly when these disciplines are clearly defined and not in a dynamic state compellingly attractive to a greater variety of adventurous souls. This situation plays an immense role in the present structure of academic politics. (Chapter 3 deals with some matters pertaining to it.)

Administration. If the remarks I have made are true, it follows that an administrator is likely to be characterized in some way by the discipline from which he emerges, although his willingness to administer sets him apart at once from most of his colleagues in that discipline. Yet knowing that discipline best, he may bend over backward to be fair to others at the expense of his own. In any case, emergence from *a* discipline is an advantage, since it gives him an inside understanding of the commitments of a faculty member, which are sometimes mysterious in their manifestations to outsiders.

As I have suggested, one of the greatest dangers to an administrator is that of becoming misanthropic with respect to faculty behavior and beginning to consider the faculty the enemy or to treat it as if it were a large, inhuman abstraction. One check against this tendency would be periodic turnover or even terms of office, as is the case in some institutions at various levels. A danger emerging from this solution might be the tendency of the administrator to identify too closely with his subject and his research during the period of his administrative duties, to the detriment of effective administration. This risk is preferable to that of leaving our institutions to professional administrators, however, although to take it means to edge up to a Principle asserting that the university must operate less efficiently at the administrative level if it is to operate more smoothly at the internal political level. (Developing the art of bureaucriticism, I shall examine administration at greater length in Chapter 7.)

IV

Fifty minutes being up, it was time for me to summarize before my friend could get out of the room. Still polite, as was required by our roles as emissaries of foreign powers, although perhaps perplexed and saddened by my exposition, he merely observed that what I had said explained a lot to him. Perhaps the reticence that I sensed in his manner, and my feeling that he thought my remarks an elaborate defense against reasonable solutions or an expression of disillusion, were only the product of the formality of our situation. Concerned, I declared that of course universities would change and that there had to be many internal reforms, that this was a time of crisis and that the whole state of education was now problematic as it had not been in my remembrance. Yet deep down inside, although I recognized the Wildean tone of my Principles and Antinomies, I assented anew to them and satisfied myself that the reforms we achieved would best be worked out with the desirability of preserving the Principles in mind. I had by this time recognized my affection for them, since I thought they illustrated that the academic world was really like the life outside it, full of apparent incompatibilities that had to be made compatible by the art of politics. I suppose that is what I had really wanted to say to my friend—

that my world was his, after all, that in some strange way my Principles were a construction designed to perform a positive act of communication, even of communion. In contrast to the self-conscious Stephen Dedalus, queried on his discussion of *Hamlet*, I had come to believe in my theory—a dangerous admission, perhaps. All the rest followed.

Chapter 2

STEREOTYPICS

ONCE HAVING LECTURED, I found myself unable to resist the professorial urge to extend my fifty minutes into a course, to elaborate my Principles, to anatomize my Antinomies, and to fill the spaces between them. An examination of the stereotyped ideas of academic life seemed to me the next order of business. But to deal with them in an orderly and academic manner it became necessary to invent a new science—stereotypics, which is the study and presentation of stereotypes from various points of view. Like most things declared to be sciences, it is, in fact, an art and requires exercise of the personal memory, willingness to ignore statistical studies, if they exist, and venting of the spleen when judiciousness threatens to distort perception. Stereotypics involves the deduction of what the eighteenth-century philosopher Giambattista Vico called "poetic universals," where the personal vision of the stereotyptician is not frittered away in logical generalizations. One can, therefore, expect to find anecdotes and self-expression in this chapter.

I

Stereotypes change slowly. The profession has had to struggle with the stereotypes of it offered by fiction, film, and itself as much as has any profession and probably more than most. Some of this agony, as I shall explain, the profession seems to bring on itself.

The Good Life Stereotype. One scene from a movie (almost everything else of which, including its title, I forget) has stuck in my mind for years. When I saw it, I was, I believe, an instructor at Cornell. The scene is a living room of a college professor and his wife. They are awaiting friends for cocktails, after which they are going to a party. Their house is large, New Englandish (perhaps Cape Cod), beautifully and expensively appointed, and spotless. The professor's wife is, of course, beautiful enough to be a movie star and coiffed accordingly. The professor is Kirk Douglas—a young Kirk Douglas. He is not old enough to be a professor of rank. He is—ha, ha—like me. And he is straightening his black tie as he goes to the door to greet his guests. He is wearing a tuxedo, and there is a silver-topped cocktail shaker on the coffee table in front of a pleasant fire. After a few moments of conversation with the guests it is apparent that Douglas is an idealist, which means a relatively free thinker—within a certain range, the boundaries of which are never tested in the dialogue. I do not remember whether the movie as a whole had any redeeming features. But it must have been rather fun to fantasize with or laugh at.

At the time it just so happens that my wife and I were living in an 1820 Greek Revival house near Ithaca, New York. That was certainly as close to Douglas's Cape Cod house as Ithaca could provide. But the difference was that we were living in two drafty rooms in the upstairs, with a closet converted to a shower, the paint of which was endlessly peeling, and a huge oil heater in the center of our larger room. What furniture came with the rent was 1920 hand-me-down. The last tux I had had—and have ever had—was one refitted from my father in the palmier days of my undergraduate life, and since discarded. My wife was working as a secretary in a Cornell office at an absurdly low salary, and I was teaching section after section of freshman English for $3,500 per year. I was lucky to have gotten any job that year.

I knew of no other young teacher in my department who was not living in about the same way. I took a job at commencement distributing caps and gowns. It had been carefully and jealously handed down from English instructor to English instructor for several years—a real plum. A colleague one Christmas signed up as a department-store Santa Claus downtown, but our chairman learned of it, took him aside, and advised him that this was not an image the department thought it well to project. He was a genius at keeping his family of a wife and three children in bread, but he went west to get tenure. Some of my colleagues, when their wives became pregnant and could not continue to hold jobs, managed to take on the mortgages of old houses and rent out rooms to make ends meet. The rest of us were at the mercy of widows who kept their own lives going by gouging young faculty for marginal housing.

This was the condition of all of us except the highest-ranking professors and those few who had private means or wives with money. (Maybe that was Kirk Douglas's game!) I believe the average full professorial salary was in the neighborhood of eight thousand dollars at the time, achieved after years of training and work. It had been worse, of course, for previous generations, in the depression; and some of our older colleagues didn't tire of letting us know this. There was also a revolving-door policy. One in four instructors was promoted to assistant professor, one in four again to tenured rank. The process, if one was successful, took ten years.

This state of affairs didn't change much until the early sixties. Then a generation of young scholars who had known neither depression, war, nor the genteel squalor of postwar faculty life might have taken Kirk Douglas in black tie as near the truth, for all that I know. I recall my own astonishment (so acclimated had I become) when in 1965 the young faculty in my new department in a new campus of the University of California rented at ages twenty-four to twenty-six whole houses—relatively new ones at that—or even *bought* them! Had something changed? Or was this just California?

Both. The houses were not, of course, Kirk Douglas's Cape Cod, or if they were, this was disguised by the addition of shag carpets, ornate hanging fixtures, Tahitian wall decorations, sunken bathtubs, and Spanish doorways. They were California speculators' assembly-line baroque, yet the stereotype persisted. Did not Taylor and Burton's *Virginia Woolf* display the conventional house?

However, affluence does not lessen the typical faculty member's capacity for achieving squalor, even amidst California newness and tawdry splendor. The way of life of the professor, with its history of penury, perpetuated itself by convention into 1965. To enter any other middle-class home and find it in such a state would be to assume that the family was going through a divorce. Generally speaking, faculty members manage obliviousness to disorder and grime and seem to have undergone lobotomy of the taste cells. Perhaps a tradition of deprivation and a certain scorn of material possessions (intrinsic to the image of the ancient peripatetic scholar-philosopher) accounts sufficiently for all this. In any case, on entering a faculty kitchen, one has to be prepared to stick to the floor, and if wearing a clean suit, dust the chair. There is danger not merely of gum on the rung but of last week's Kool-Aid on the seat. Not much has changed even today. Beware also of young children and cats—beneath, above, and to the side.

The Detached Life Stereotype. The movie probably didn't tell us very much about how Kirk Douglas carried on his academic life, except that he stood for truth and integrity and had to deal with mendacity. But it can be shown that the media stereotype of the professor is that of the detached life. The college is the isolated small community. TV in-depth reports begin by showing coeds walking down tree-lined paths, even though they may shift to protesters or freaks. This convention has much to do with pastoral tradition; it is about as ideal as Kirk Douglas in his tux. It is connected with the treatment of professors as absent-minded, pleasantly eccentric, ineffective in public situations, and so forth. There do exist a sufficient number of professors of this sort to perpetuate the myth. The archetype here is not Douglas but James Stewart in his more dithering moments.

It is not too much to say that this deeply ingrained myth of detachment contributed strongly to the shock of Governor Ronald Reagan at the academic behavior he saw in the University of California in the sixties. It had been a long time since the Berkeley campus had been like the tree-sprinkled bucolic small colleges far to the east. And as for Berkeley professors, there didn't seem to be a Jimmy Stewart in the lot. Governor Reagan had much difficulty coming to terms with the real existence of Clark Kerr, and set about exorcising the demon, only to discover that Kerr's successor spent more time in places like Washington, D.C.—and had more experience in government—than he did, besides presiding over what in itself had become a huge and complex political entity.

The myth of detachment could no longer be believed in by faculty members who had to deal with the campuses of the sixties, and some were exhilarated by the new pace. But, of course, it was not really *that* new. Professors, as we all now know, had already become globe-hoppers and industrial consultants to an unprecedented extent. But myths do persist, and even this one did, while the universities were coming to be more like huge retirement cities for adolescents, replete with problems of crime, crowding, and boredom.

In 1962–63 I was a Fulbright lecturer at Trinity College,

Dublin, on leave from Michigan State University. When I left State in 1962 its enrollment was about 20,000. When I returned it had grown to about 26,000. I am told it has reached to 40,000 since. At Trinity one evening, after presiding at the debating society founded by Edmund Burke (the subject was "Resolved, that Columbus should have stayed at home"!) I was asked by a participant how large my university was. I told him, and his immediate response was to ask, "What do you do about crime?" I had never thought of it as a problem, but then I reflected that a few days before leaving the campus I had tried to help out a young man from Detroit who had gotten himself involved with people in a narcotics sale. Enrollment had sneaked up on me, just as slyly as the new General Motors Gothic buildings at State were mushrooming and driving the horses, pigs, and pastoral cattle ever southward from the Red Cedar River. Some part of me had held on to the stereotype, though the shepherds had long since departed.

The Nonlife Stereotype. One myth that is never actually spoken but must exist in the freshman ken like some unobservable planet drains the faculty member of essential life. There is nothing ideal about this myth. It is not a cold pastoral vision, though the resulting image of the faculty member has some of the ghostliness of an essence or Platonic form. I deduce this unspoken myth in the basin of the freshman brain from observation of phenomena that require it for an explanation. In this vision the faculty member is a pure presence rather than a being-in-the-world. He has no spouse, no child, no dog, no cat, no home. He may be seen entering a car, but he disappears into nothingness when he leaves the range of the naked eye. He does not sleep or eat. Either he is in his office or his classroom or he is nowhere. If one calls him on the phone, one is calling just his number, not a home, not a place where there is life but only one where there is *information* and *authority.* It is possible to call him at 2 P.M. or 2 A.M. He is either a voice at the other end or he is not. If his sleepy wife answers, it is the wrong number. Faculty have, in short, a special mode of existence (like a work of art? No, like a computer). If they are not in their offices at exactly the prescribed time they are out of order, and the chairman should fix them at once.

The Absurd Life Stereotype. The stereotypes of academic life as seen from the outside have for some time been matched by the stereotype created inside. The academic novel, usually written by a professor of English, is most often satire, sometimes farce, and often a symbolic act of revenge against a world that has turned out to be different from what has been advertised. Morris Bishop's *Widening Stain* is a good-natured farce—a *roman à clef* having to do with murder in the (barely disguised) old Cornell library. Mary McCarthy's *Groves of Academe* is perhaps the best-known satirical novel of the genre. I am told that Randall Jarrell's less famous *Pictures from an Institution* is a response. Academic novelists like to put colleagues into their books and answer colleagues in their books. But serious treatments are rare. The English professor's penchant as a creative writer seems to be for wit and satire, as eavesdropping in the departmental office during coffee hour will quickly reveal. The attitude toward the situation he and his colleagues are all in is probably best expressed by an excellent quip I have heard attributed to Professor Mark Schorer, that the academic profession is a parody of a lost original. A serious novel with an academic setting is likely to be treated as satire in spite of itself. In my own *Horses of Instruction* (1968) there is a satirical attitude, but it is expressed by one of the narrators and occasionally by another. I felt that this attitude was appropriate to those characters but not necessary to the novel as a whole, but reviewers tended to see only the satirical. My point is that their approach expresses an attitude common also within the profession—one of the few which it is *de rigueur* to berate publicly and from the inside. In part this is the result of the paranoia that the profession seems to generate within itself. Curiously, the tendency to berate is not by any means confined to professors but has become one of the acceptable styles among administrators. This is perhaps the result of the bureaucratization of the cry for change in the sixties. Thus, unless the administrator speaks warmly of innovation and change in the face of the intransigence of the bureau itself (and often the faculty), his statement is ritualistically incomplete. From the back page of the *Chronicle of Higher Education*, some professor or administrator weekly criticizes the profession and helps make his reputation as a go-getter. A magazine of education spawned in the sixties is called *Change*—all of which, as they say in *1066 and All That* is regarded as a *Good Thing*, no matter how mindlessly those verbal beads are counted.

A good many of these critical statements are merely cashings-in on the fashion. But in any case, both the external and the internal stereotype emerge from similar idealistic pictures. The difference lies in the fact that the latter criticizes the reality for falling short, while the former in its persistence resists abandoning the pastoral vision of the university even in times of stress.

The Political Stereotype. Many years ago the treasurer of the board of trustees of the school of which my father was headmaster asked my father why the faculty members were apparently almost unanimously Democrats. My father did not argue with that assessment (I believe he himself, though not, I think, a socialist, had voted for Norman Thomas at about this time—1936). There were, in fact, some Republicans on the faculty. He replied craftily (but without effect) that if his teachers were paid more there might be some conversions. Apparently this concept was beyond the capacities of the treasurer, a man of brilliance when his own funds were at stake but cautious sometimes to imbecility with the school's. There was some truth to my father's rejoinder, but he was using it more than professing it.

The cry that faculties are politically unbalanced has been coming from sources external to the universities for years. The most recent example has been the emergence of a right-wing magazine designed to compete with the official *Princeton Alumni Weekly*, whose relentless reminders of one's continuing attachment to the university cease only in the summer months. The new magazine is the voice of the self-proclaimed Concerned Alumni of Princeton, and is called *Prospect*, a title which in itself points to an ominous future and recalls a glorious past when the Prospect Street eating clubs were taken as very much more important than they are today. This magazine attacks the Princeton administration for its admissions policy, including suspected quotas for minority students, the advent of coeducation, the increase in campus crime, the decline of the honor system, the eclipse of football fortunes, the abolition of ROTC, the demise of several eating clubs, everybody's behavior in the sixties, and most vigorously the alleged almost total absence of political conservatives on the Princeton faculty, particularly in the so-called social sciences. In every issue we are shown lists of assigned readings, reports of lectures, and the results of polls, all serving to illustrate this last complaint. The magazine has taken away some of the amusement of the *Alumni Weekly*, since the most cantankerous letters from graduates now tend to appear in *Prospect*, where the writers think they have a true friend. At the same time, liberals write in outrage, attacking the magazine. The *Weekly*'s letters seem to have become more bland. It almost appears that having missed the chance to let off steam in the previous decade, the conservatives are having their vicarious sixties in print.

The external stereotype is perhaps true enough. I do not

have before me the conclusions of Ladd and Lipset, who have
studied this matter. (Besides, I have vowed to eschew statistics and keep to my own impressions, to say nothing of preju-
dices.) I am sure that the liberal preponderance increases as
we examine progressively each level of education from primary school to university. I do not know the figures for the
faculty of Princeton or any other university. *Prospect* cites, I
believe, a faculty vote on the Vietnam war and a straw vote
in the Nixon-McGovern election; some letter writers have
pointed out that these votes may only reflect the intelligence
of the faculty, not political persuasion. *Prospect* does not seem
to grasp the possibility that the country has been in the midst
of a political realignment that renders certain labels obsolete,
especially among intellectuals, and that academic intellectuals
often on principle take independent stances and play the role
of the reprobate. But, of course, in the stereotypical view intellectuals are probably even more suspect than liberals of
perpetrating outrages against society and common sense. I do
not believe that I know of any one in my department who has
consistently voted Republican—at least anyone who admits
it. This does not mean that everyone votes Democratic or
would admit it. The situation, I am told, is different in the
professional schools—medicine, business, engineering, and
the like. But with respect to the heart of the university the
situation *Prospect* deplores at Princeton but does not fully understand probably prevails at virtually all major American
universities. In another age it may have been different. I can
imagine earlier in the century—very early—a preponderance
of Republican voters, but I doubt very much that this pre-
vented the same sorts of suspicion of professors and intellectuals generally. That seems inevitable, and in any case people
attracted to the academic profession are likely to be interested
in ideas. Ideas that attract the most interest are new ideas.
Therefore . . .

Conservatism has been the politics of business and commerce. Academics are more free of the tendency to identify business and commerce with their immediate self-interest than perhaps any other group. Indeed, their self-interest (when they are in state universities, at least) seems to be with the Democrats because it is the Republicans who have traditionally formed the majority of those who vote against their salary increases and various other university budget requests. This fact alone does not seem, however, to be the dominating element in the matter, since private institutions apparently have at least as large a so-called liberal faculty majority as public institutions. Another significant element could be that research funds are alleged to be easier to obtain from the federal government under Democratic regimes. But here again, political affiliation and this sort of self-interest seem to me less significant than the attitude of the academic individual toward ideas and the teacher's role.

Then there is the argument that intense liberal education leads away from conservatism toward liberal (in the political sense) and radical politics. This is by no means proved. To be sure, in recent years I have seen surveys that indicate that this observation is now correct. But for years higher education seemed to have little effect on the political attitudes of students, and presumably in those days proportionally more of them were taking so-called liberal-arts majors. This is a big and complex subject, and I do not have the information necessary to pursue it, but I am willing to believe that fundamentally the political stereotype is a product of general suspicion of the intellectual on the grounds of his strangeness and freedom.

Doctrinaire union officials, members of the unions' rank and file, and radicals have found the academic intellectual as obnoxious as does the editor of *Prospect*. And not just during the period of student rebellion. Let us face it, there is something funny about *us*. A good many years ago I was playing shortstop for a city league softball team and had managed to keep my connection with the university a secret from my teammates. But eventually (not coincident with a batting slump) the question of what I did was asked, and I was truthful. The response of the questioner was that he had *thought* there was something funny about me. But then gradually, my teammates seemed to develop a curious pride in my presence. I was harmlessly unusual. I was, after that, "Doc" or "Prof." Still, I may be the only player in the history of baseball who was actually assaulted by an umpire, for what I, at least, regarded as a very mild demurrer. Perhaps *he* had found out.

All freedom is dangerous, as Joyce Cary pointed out. Cary said he did not fear for freedom so much as he feared what man would do with it. The relative freedom of the academic (at the higher levels of his trade) is related to the myth of the good life—the academic pastoral. The friendly businessman one knows slightly speaks from time to time of a suppressed desire to teach, or an intention to teach when he retires, or he looks wistfully at the time he has lost when he could have been thinking or reading and generally improving his mind. In this mood he admires the pastoral vision at a discreet and respectful distance.

But this is not always the prevailing mood. Stories in academic life of the persecution of academics from the outside for alleged leftist political views are legion, and many are true. The loyalty-oath controversy in California was regarded as an example of this, and the Canwell Committee activity at the University of Washington in the late forties is an infamous case. Three professors at Washington were then dismissed because of membership in the Communist party. I had been a student of two of them. Neither could in any conceivable way have been rationally accused of teaching either directly or surreptitiously a communistic position. Another professor, not a party member, had been interpreting American literature in a Marxist way for years, and was never involved. I can't say that he harmed his students more or less than other teachers. Many of us were probably more radical than he at that time anyway, and no doubt we condescended to him. In any case, on their own grounds the inquisitors got the wrong men.

External persecution of so-called conservatives is extremely rare, from my experience, in academic life. The only case I know, and a mild and absurd one at that, occurred in the thirties when a committee from the state legislature (very militantly Democratic) visited my father's school for some purpose related to accreditation. That day the son of a very conservative local doctor had brought some books to our history teacher in the hope of showing him the light. These were on his desk when the legislators visited, and this teacher got very low marks until my father protested. In fact, this teacher was a parlor socialist and regarded as quite a radical by the students. Of course, when the student straw vote came out at *my* school, I was for a whole month convinced that Landon would defeat Roosevelt. Our teacher wasn't able to pierce the armor of conservatism that surrounded most of the students.

II

The terms "liberal" and "conservative" (to say nothing of "radical") cause a great deal of confusion when applied anywhere, but particularly when external political attitudes are equated with internal campus politics or with educational theory. It would be pleasant, to say nothing of symmetrical, to declare Principle the First of Stereotypics to be that a political liberal is an academic conservative and vice versa. Though examples of this can be found by virtue of the preponderance of political liberals on campuses, the idea cannot rise to the level of a Principle. Instead, the Principle of random behavior seems to reign.

From the very beginning, it must be understood that a liberal education has little, if anything, to do with either liberal or conservative politics. If in the past a liberal education has been anything, it has been one professing to conserve a cultural heritage, but with an open mind, therefore transcendent of or inclusive of the clichés of both sides. Because of its interest in the past—in history and in the literature and philosophy of the past—it has been subject inside academe to fairly incessant oblique attack from the social sciences (when they have been ahistorical) and other disciplines where "methodology" has become a catchword. This conflict is the source of a profound division in academic and intellectual life generally and does not at all express a division along external political lines. It does lead to charges of reaction leveled against the liberal-arts departments, and elicits a general attitude among those departments that the social and applied sciences are areas of cultural barbarism. Usually this attitude is alleged merely to be snobbishness by the recipients, but the repartee only increases the division. It avoids the intellectual issue at the source, rarely debated university-wide. To debate an intellectual issue might well lead actually to arguing *against* one's own shorter-term budgetary interests—an appalling prospect to any dean or chairman. One example may here suffice. It has to do with the matter of requirements. Academic requirements tend to wax and wane according to some pattern not yet worked out rudimentarily even in astrology. The debate on the right number and kind of academic requirements takes on the character of medieval theological dispute. Two Principles are certain. (1) *Debate over requirements deteriorates rapidly from the level of principle to that of expediency.* (2) *Debate over requirements deteriorates more rapidly the higher the level of administration at which the debate is carried on.*

These are Principles of Stereotypics, since they tend to stereotype academic behavior according to personal experience. I have actually heard quite sensible discussions of academic requirements in the relative privacy of faculty offices and even in the hallways and the cafeteria. I have rarely heard sense spoken about this matter in a committee of a faculty senate, and chairmen and deans meeting together are hardly willing to discuss it at all, perhaps on the reasonable assumption that they will inevitably appear to be hypocrites if they do. But also there is a great lack of conviction about these questions that leads to a convenient cynicism.

During the great enrollment boom, the development of new programs, and the student unrest of the 1960s, there was a tendency passively to erase academic requirements which were beyond departmental control. One of the first to go was the foreign-language requirement (some say as a courtesy to the football coach); next, freshman composition. The science requirement, if not abandoned, was often made more flexible, and so on. But none of these moves occurred totally on educational grounds. Foreign-language departments had enough students in the bonanza years as it was; so did English departments. Space in labs was at a premium. And then there is the stereotypical Principle of behavior which says that (3) *an educational principle is fine as long as it does not interfere with a departmental program.* This Principle was well illustrated for me during the planning year at my own California campus. And it is here I must demonstrate that the science of stereotypics is an art, complete with invective and bias, for to offer my illustration I must express my own sense of the proper nature of liberal education and lament what seems stereotypically to have happened to it (if it ever existed) in the light of the three Principles I have enunciated. In what follows I think of so-called humanistic study as the foundation, but by no means all—only the beginning—of a liberal education.

First, a little history of what has happened to humanists. In the late fifties and early sixties, immense support, largely from the federal government, came to institutions of higher education for purposes of advanced scientific research and training of new researchers. The result was an unparalleled emphasis on specialized learning and the increased autonomy of particular disciplines. The disciplines receiving this support defined their aim as the production of highly competent professional specialists devoted to their subjects. The model of learning became the doctorate in some area of the natural sciences. As the sixties staggered to their conclusion, a reaction set in against this sort of higher education, as it seemed to set in against everything else. We all know that dissatisfactions tied up with the Vietnam war and domestic social problems affected the universities, and there is no need to rehearse them here. It is well, however, to understand that the model of learning generated principally by federal support has been changing, not simply because students cried "relevance" and opposed "war research," but also because governmental interest itself has shifted to other problems. In this transitional stage, the confusion and anxiety of the academic community has been the result not merely of tighter budgets but also of the shifting of academic power and authority. The physicists have had to adjust to a relatively diminished role. The biologists were and are bullish. The social scientists are elated or depressed according to their various faiths in their ability to deal with critical social problems.

Governmental policy now presses for greater emphasis on vocational training. The cry is heard everywhere—from legislative halls to school-board meetings. It is a reassertion of pragmatic values, of that stereotypical anti-intellectualism which lies deep in the American grain. From one point of view, this trend should not affect the stance of the humanities and the definition of the ideal of liberal education (if there is one), but in fact the stance of the humanities has been shaky ever since the role of government in education increased.

It is clear that in the late fifties, humanists—those who teach the literatures, literary theory, language, history, or philosophy—began to ape their far more affluent scientific colleagues. Intensive specialization in research led to a hardening of departmental boundaries, which was helped along by the immense growth of academic institutions and accom-

panying problems of communication among administrative
units. Some departments became so large that they could
hardly be expected to have much to do with any others, even
those intellectually close to them. There appeared in increasing numbers the entrepreneurial humanist, a pale copy of his
more mobile, affluent scientist colleague, but nevertheless
having absorbed by osmosis a taste for the heady delights of
travel to international meetings, reduced teaching loads, exclusively graduate teaching, and whatever opportunities in
grantsmanship developed in his field. Teaching in the humanities, too, turned toward emphasis on the production of advanced degrees, with concentration on a particular subject
matter. Programs for undergraduates narrowed as the model
of the successful undergraduate in a humanistic discipline became, as it was in the sciences, the person achieving a bache-
lor's degree leading to graduate study. Of course, this shift in
emphasis had been going on less perceptibly somewhat earlier, but suddenly it speeded up. Few people in academic life
have really reflected on how far we have gone in this direction
and how far the humanities, and with them the ideal of a liberal education, have slipped from their central place in the
curriculum of the university. Most academics are themselves
products of the trend.

   In an interesting way, the physical design of the campus
where I teach reflects this phenomenon. Somewhat ironically,
but nonetheless affectionately, called "instant university"
when we began classes in 1965 (on the very crest of the affluent movement I have mentioned), my own campus was laid
out in a huge circle, with a park at the center and five of the
major schools located around it—Humanities, Biological
Sciences, Physical Sciences, Engineering, and Social Sciences. The School of Fine Arts stands outside of the circle
itself, behind Humanities; the College of Medicine, behind
Biological Sciences. Between Humanities and Social Sciences stands the Library.

One could devise a number of images to represent this design—a huge pie divided into wedges, spokes on a wheel, and so forth. None of them, in my opinion, places the humanities in their appropriate symbolic role in a university. None offers a symbolic vision of a liberal education. The physical plan has either influenced or mirrored the way the roles of the various schools have been defined. One might indeed say that the physical plan has set the concept of the humanities in concrete. I do not see how any humanist who has tried seriously to define the humanities to himself as they *ought* to be could be content to imagine them as a spoke on the wheel of learning or as a slice of a pie, but the concept is not in any way peculiar to my own institution. The imagery grew, of course, from the national trend toward disciplinary definition and research specialization. The *nature* of the academic plan copied the *art* of the architect. But the architect reflected the temper of the times. I recall, in 1964, certain people in rather high places, who commanded some respect in my institution, raising questions—often in the form of oracular statements—about the importance of a library to a really modern campus. It was, after all, principally the humanists who needed all those books; the rest of the faculty and students would be using information-retrieval systems, and the humanists were, after all, only one spoke on the wheel, had only one slice of the pie, and were rather stuck in the past to boot. While some physicists and chemists I know have begun to refer to the time when remarks such as those were being made as the good old days, I am less sentimental.

It was during this period that what must have been some manifestation of collective academic and political guilt brought about the creation of the National Endowment for the Humanities. During the post-Sputnik years, the role of the humanities had diminished significantly in the curriculum of the university student, as the requirements themselves were discarded. The humanities had, indeed, come to be regarded as one spoke on the wheel of learning. With fresh-man English, first reduced to a "skill," disappearing from the list of mandated courses, and foreign-language requirements already nearly gone, the humanities became largely a collec-tion of "cultural" addenda to the apparently real business of learning. Under these circumstances, the National Endow-ment for the Humanities, the support for which was minus-cule by comparison to the sums poured into science, in some ways enforced the mirror image of the sciences that some *au courant* humanists had already adopted in other ways. Hu-manists competed for the Endowment's resources, began to write grant proposals, and traveled to give lectures; a few found ways to go to Europe and even India. But something was wrong, because the humanities, whatever they are, are not the sciences; and very little has been done, aside from repetition of the usual utterances about value, to try to under-stand what the humanities are or can be.

The good—or bad—old days are gone, unlikely to return. Few humanists can suppress a wry smile at their physicist friends' discovery of anxiety. Humanists have never really been on the gravy train, though some have comically mim-icked the riders, and it is unlikely that they ever will be. Some may have basked from time to time in the glory of the mime's role. After all, the jester and the poet both once had the king's ear. But, as Yeats says about an unrequited love of his youth, "Now it seems an idle trade enough."

I like to think that perhaps the humanists are all coming to their senses. I notice that diminishment of enrollments in their courses has led many to loud complaints about illiter-acy, somehow unnoticed until the enrollment crisis hit. Ah well, any port in a storm! They now face an external threat that must be balanced against their own self-destructive ten-dencies toward isolation, narrow specialization, and purity. The threat may yet save them. The cry abroad in the land is not for research and higher degrees nor for "relevance," whatever *that* was. Instead it is for vocational training and career preparation in strictly the narrowest sense. La Belle Dame Sans Merci is beckoning again. I have been around long enough to recognize that old witch. It is the witch who beckoned the World War II veterans and later the aerospace people, who now beckons so many children into biology. I wonder· how many expect to make fabulous money as physicians, own big cars and houses, and join the right golf clubs, even perhaps get into the proprietary health-care business. What will they do when they discover that the medical schools are full and the profession is overcrowded or, to be more precise, artificially limited in size? What will happen to these people when, faced with the necessity of improvisation, they have not read anything, cannot read well, cannot write, and have never made connections with a past that might have provided them with some perspective on their situation?

In a way, we have already experienced the angst of one such generation brought up without history. The young are very quick to perceive what is wrong, quicker than they are at understanding how to make it right or how hard it is to make it right or that earlier people have really tried or that some things can't be quite right. The young of recent times came to a massive spiritual agreement that something was wrong. Yet they were the product of what was wrong themselves. The student movement—associated with war protest and drugs—turned quickly into a historically familiar mode of negative romanticism and then decadence. I saw it coming when I realized that middle-class youths were beginning to dig Shelley and Byron. Soon, of course, they dug nothing but their own thing.

Was all of this collapse of discipline and dismissal of the intellect the proper antidote to overspecialization and the graduate-school model of learning? No, it was not. It was itself a negation, not a proper contrary, as William Blake would have said. So everyone experimented with techniques. People rapped in all conceivable physical positions, abandoned chairs for pillows or the floor, assembled around coffeepots and in kiva-like rooms or in grassy nooks, changed clothing, eyeglasses, faces; soon one couldn't even recognize one's close acquaintances. None of it worked, and for many it was depressing. The incidence of breakdown increased markedly among students and faculty alike. Romanticism had again become decadence, but like everything else in our lives, the whole process had speeded up immensely. Yet most of the individuals to whom this was happening hadn't known about all those people with all those problems so long ago. Some will say the whole process was necessary or inevitable—a vast purgation. The point is too general to be argued—or argued with. It is clearly more important to determine what is necessary so that individuals can obtain the resources to remove themselves from this sort of cyclic anxiety. It would help to look at undergraduate higher education and at the model of it. The model of the wheel or the pie is wrong. At this point I want to introduce a large and inclusive stereotype, generated from within, inasmuch as I am an academic, and designed to replace the horizontal or circular stereotype that has governed academic thought for too long. The proper arrangement of the disciplines in higher education is vertical, not horizontal, with the proviso that before we tilt the whole plan we recognize that without a good substructure the totality will crash into ruin.

At the bottom of this hierarchical structure are the humanities and the fine arts, and a little higher up is mathematics. The humanities ought to be regarded as the mode of learning by which we individually and collectively attempt to recover, maintain, keep flexible, analyze, and criticize the verbal culture in which we live. Few of us reflect as much as we might on the degree to which we inhabit a world made up of words, to what extent we are, in Ernst Cassirer's words, an *animal symbolicum*. As soon as our minds and feelings begin to develop, we grow into a verbal universe. To understand this statement, one has only to imagine what our lives would be like if we were not language-making creatures. We certainly wouldn't live in the world we now live in; the world of science, constructed on top of language as we have evolved it, would not exist, for the special form of language we call mathematics would not have come into being. It is *in* language, for example, that we construct the past. Blake says that the second coming of Jesus occurs in the words of the Bible—that is, our reading of the Bible brings Jesus into the present. So with all history. We like to think of the past as somewhere *back there*, so to speak, but in fact, it is here and now in the language in which historians create it for us. The past, even in the informal histories our parents and elders pass on to us, is principally verbal, and in its various forms it is utterly necessary to us.

The present is a surrounding world of words complete with that verbally constructed past. Each of us struggles to control and understand it. Living generations are the most self-bombarded by verbal symbols of any in history. The various media slaughter language more rapidly and thoroughly than at any time in the past. It is true, of course, that men in other generations have viewed the state of the verbal universe with alarm. Witness Wordsworth in 1800: "A multitude of causes, unknown to former times, are now acting with a combined force to blunt the discriminating powers of the mind, and, unfitting it for all voluntary exertion, to reduce it to a state of almost savage torpor." One would almost think Wordsworth was writing about the week's TV schedule. More than ever, more than in Wordsworth's time, new generations will have to be careful how they digest what is offered them verbally—by advertisers, politicians, and self-appointed gurus. Language is always dying from such use, even as it must be continually rebuilt. The rebuilding is necessary unless the culture is to deaden in intellect and spirit. If the rebuilding ceases, the vocabulary that George Orwell called "Newspeak" in his novel *Nineteen Eighty-four* will become the verbal reality, and human beings will have become slaves to it. What we call the art of literature has always been the creation of that part of the verbal universe most concerned with intellectual flexibility and new possibilities. It therefore belongs somewhere near the base of our vertical structure. Shelley wrote, "If no new poets should arise to create afresh the associations which have been . . . disorganized, language will be dead to all the nobler purposes of human intercourse." Among "poets," Shelley included not only the makers of so-called poems but philosophers and historians. He saw the poet, in this sense, as one who constantly tests and experiments with the possibilities of language, trying to refurbish it, even as the devourers render whole portions of it dead, language being fragile and tending toward cliché. Literary study is the observation of such efforts, the discussion of them, and to a great extent, the recovery and preservation of those verbal shapes of the past that retain the power to generate thought anew. These works are popularly called "classics." We return to them not because they are entertaining—though they may well be—but because thought can build upon them. Thus, as I have suggested, they stand at the base of human learning. The historian, using the language of the past as his primary material, constructs a presence of the past in language. The linguist searches out systems of language use. The philosopher uses and examines language to test the validity of ideas and to generate new systems of thought.

The verbal universe is a set of symbols in which human beings express the moral imagination. Human beings are distinguished to a great extent by their conscious aspirations, their capacity to have desires and to formulate them verbally. What they seek is thus subject to critique and refinement, but most important, the formulated desire becomes part of their reality—as desire—in a way impossible to other creatures. This is true of the opposite of desire as well—what Professor Northrop Frye has called the "limit of repugnance." This world of desire and its opposite, building and constantly decaying in the forms of language, is the humanist's concern. He sees it as the verbal emanation of man and the barrier between man and chaos. When that world threatens to become mute and confused, he seeks to repair it, to recover the still-useful verbal power of the past and encourage the verbal arts of the present.

Each of us, as he grows up, makes a verbal universe for himself and inherits some parts of the verbal universe that surrounds him. Not many of us add anything of lasting value to the whole, though some of us make careers trying. It is at worst a harmless occupation compared to assaulting the environment thoughtlessly with automobiles, bulldozers, and the like. At the least, each of us must live in the verbal universe, working out problems words create, telling the better from the worse, and responding with words. So humanistic teaching as a part of liberal education should involve preparing people to do these things—to discriminate and choose, to employ language, if not creatively, at least clearly, if only to avoid boredom or confusion in the mind of the reader or listener. Some thought may be prelinguistic, as we are told today, but most of it occurs in human transactions with symbolic systems, by which what is only potential is brought into existence. Thus humanistic study is not primarily meant to make professionals, though some students choose that road. Rather it is fundamental to the education of everyone, the basis of a liberal education, and essential to an effective citizenry.

As such, the study of the humanities cannot properly exist as a spoke on the wheel of learning, for it is at the foundation of learning. I do *not* mean that humanists must be revered above all other teachers or that such study must therefore *precede* all other learning temporally in the education of an individual. A certain amount of it must do so, of course, but humanistic learning is not a skill to be mastered *in order to* proceed to a higher skill. It is a continuous process, like life itself.

This brings me finally to an example, or stereotypical anecdote, illustrating the principles I have stated. In 1964, when my own institution was in the academic planning stage, I attended a series of meetings of deans and chairmen and a few newly appointed faculty that composed the advance guard, so to speak, for the program to be launched in 1965. Some of the ideas developed in those meetings require scrutiny today in the light of my preceding remarks. These ideas are common in the thinking of educators all over the country, and thus discussion of them can help us to understand the problem of liberal education generally.

First, it was concluded that we should award credit to students for "accomplishment" rather than for courses attended and passed. This was to be a principle of universal application. It would include the granting of credit in, say, expository writing if the student could prove that he could write adequately according to some standard of competence. It was to be called "credit by examination." I have no objection to this as a principle of limited applicability. But I now regard it as of little value in the humanities. The reason is partly that no one ever comes to believe he writes well enough unless he has what, in my opinion, is an inadequate measure of desire. Thus, in my view, the teaching of writing is simply a continuing process for which credit is an illusion and competence an inadequate term. The only solution here to meeting the needs of the culture is for each student continually to be required to write—through his entire academic career under the supervision of a hard taskmaster who knows a lot about the pedagogy of writing. Recently I heard a colleague complain that a certain pedagogical idea sounded too "schoolmasterish." I don't really think that I ever had a good teacher who wasn't schoolmasterish, often in the extreme. The writing of a student in the university should be frequent, thoroughly analyzed by a schoolmasterish taskmaster, and fully integrated into his total academic program for the full extent of his stay at the university.

Second, at those meetings in 1964, it was universally acclaimed that every student should take freshman English, or expository writing. Universally acclaimed, that is, except by the chairman of English, who was at that time myself. I argued that I was not really interested in having students poured into my department by a universal requirement. Too large a portion of these people would come to us from advisors in their schools who, when asked why the requirement existed, would answer that they really didn't know, it wasn't their idea, the student just had to take the course. I argued that if the assembled deans and chairmen thought it was so important for their students to write well, they should include the requirement as part of their own programs, within the number of credits they were allowed to stipulate. Faced with a rather liberal limit on the number of credits they could stipulate (but faced also in some cases by standards for majors set by national societies in their specializations), no department or school elected to require freshman English.

I now regret my flight of candor and regard it as the result of an overwhelming urge toward perversity. I had disregarded the fact that in that group, it was simply assumed that writing was a skill which one learned, as one learns to strip down a Chevvy. (This idea had long ago invaded even English departments. Witness the term "writer's workshop.") That is nonsense, as anyone with educational experience should understand. My mistake grew from my lack of faith in the ability of English departments to achieve the end desired by offering freshman English as a "skill" course to be passed *through*. The problem of teaching writing is the problem not of teaching a skill, but of providing a continuous humanistic education through the whole of the college career. A stopgap method, which is what a "skill" course is in this case, won't work. The model is wrong. The faculty must decide finally whether or not a humanistic foundation for an education is important and why, and if they decide it is, must act accordingly by sustaining it through the students' whole college career and devising ways in which work in the sciences and social sciences is referable back to it.

I had also disregarded Principle the Third of Stereotypics, that an educational principle is fine as long as it does not interfere with a departmental program. But all principles do!

Third, we adopted a general campus "breadth requirement," which has proved less and less sensible each year but about which we seem unable to do anything. The so-called 6-3-3 requirement was our tip of the hat to *general* education—not *liberal* or *basic* education—but *general* education. The catalogue speaks as follows:

> Rather than prescribing specific courses or areas, the faculty simply states that a given portion of a student's work should be in areas outside his major. This requirement may be met by taking course work through schools or, by petition, work in Interschool Curricula programs, in Engineering, or in undergraduate courses taught in the Graduate School of Administration, outside the School of the student's major, as follows:
>
> A student must take *six* courses outside his major in one school and *three* courses in each of two other schools outside his major.

As I have indicated, this can only be regarded as a *general* education requirement, since any course in any unit fulfills it and no courses are specifically designated as appropriate. Furthermore, it is a general education requirement with a vengeance. It takes the word "general" literally, placing no responsibility on any unit to offer courses appropriate to any conceivable vision of liberal or basic education. Indeed, by af-

terthought I can only conclude that adoption of the requirement was based upon a mixture of three things: the lack of
agreed-upon educational policy transcending that of the departments (where individual policies were often well worked
out) in the group as a whole, the carrying into action of my
three Principles, and some convenient faulty analogical thinking. The requirement was adopted without any debate over
the difference between general and liberal education. Academic politics played a role as a result of the division of the
academic program according to a model reflecting the physical layout, which itself seems to have been devised to reflect
the current academic fashion. On the basis of that model,
each academic unit seemed to deserve an equal slice of the
pie. The deans and chairmen voting in concert naturally
agreed to divide things equitably among the schools—the pie
consisting of the students, of course. Enrollments generate
faculty, space, and support dollars. Because this group was
principally composed of administrators, my second Principle
applied. The 6-3-3 requirement ensured three things: that no
unit would be shut off from the opportunity to attract students, that students would take work outside of their schools,
and that each student would have to take at least three
courses in a science. The fundamental reason cited in behalf
of the requirement was that it encouraged students to explore
fields outside their own. "Encouragement" was the word.
The cry across the land was that students were adults and
should not be coerced. Of course, it was all right to coerce
them with respect to work in their majors. Coercion became
intolerable only when *liberal* education became coercive!

The convenient faulty analogical thinking to which I refer
took the form of the idea, expressed here and there early in
our discussion, that the university was a sort of supermarket
in which the student filled up his shopping cart with courses.
It was assumed that the student knew best, or ought to know
best, what he should take—beyond his major. The analogy is

a very bad one—an example of decayed language and thus subject to humanistic critique. I shall refrain from extending it all the way to absurdity except to remark that in a super-market, the real meat is prohibitively priced, while in a university, the real courses cost no more than the trivial ones. It was convenient because it left everything open to competition and no one seemed to be in anyone's way. Its absurdity has recently become more obvious, with the creation of new academic units that don't fit the requirement and are clamoring for their piece of the pie. Tinkering with the requirement goes on, but effecting change is as difficult as trying to rewrite a state constitution. I might add that the first faculty member I ever heard use the supermarket analogy became a vice-president.

I do not wish to be too hard on those of us who sat at those original planning meetings. We did very well in many ways, and I am proud of a lot that has happened in my institution. And there is no doubt we were all honorable men. Some considered our institution the university of the future and the humanities a thing of the past. But to study the past is not to belong to it, but to assert one's difference from it and connections to it. Competition among ourselves, and *our own specialized training*, ruled our behavior to a considerable degree, and we were not prepared to respond to doubts about our various rules.

The kind of breadth requirement we adopted, as I have indicated, might be defended as an encouragement toward general education that exercises the least possible amount of coercion. It has the virtue of making it possible for a student to do many things. But it encourages nothing in the faculty and expresses no sense of the aim of a liberal education. After all, as I have suggested, almost anything can belong to "general education," if we take the term literally. For that very reason, the term has always seemed to me unfortunate. By contrast, "liberal education" has always carried the emphasis of freeing and expanding the mind rather than offering a little information here and a little there. General education can live with the symbol of the academic pie, for it is a horizontal idea; but liberal education requires a hierarchical image, and humanistic study finds its place at the base. The fundamental liberal study for man is attention to his own symbolic forms of expression, primarily the world of words, or verbal culture, but also other symbolic forms—mathematics and the fine arts. The old song put into bare language a very fundamental concept of education—reading, writing, and 'rithmetic. The execution may not have been very sophisticated, but no one has shown that these disciplines are not fundamental. The problem, of course, is that they have been regarded as skills to be learned rather than worlds constantly to be made and in which to live.

No institution I know of has ever had a curriculum, a set of requirements, or a delineation of courses offered to the student that is specifically meant to continue what should be the student's endless striving to understand and contribute to the verbal culture. If we could simply define liberal education as at the base of our vertical structure—not, however, as something that one *completes* in order to proceed further—it would not be necessary constantly to devise excuses for education that either consist of just so many words or offer only examples of immediate practical use. If, for example, one wants to make better citizens, one does not begin by announcing that particular aim, because doing so leads too easily to the invention by dunces of so-called shortcuts to patriotism. Instead one must help the student along the road to understanding and coping with the verbal culture.

The problem of humanities faculties is partly the result of their self-defeating parody of the scientists, narrow specialization, and the open marketplace of competition among humanistic disciplines. The humanities lack an effective definition of their educational task, and most other definitions are too easy. But humanists can no longer be content with a slice of the pie; they should not regard themselves as a spoke on the wheel of learning. The situation which allowed that comfortable existence has changed. But it was never right. I do not know whether any humanistic faculty can change its curriculum or itself rapidly enough to save itself and humane learning in the academy. It would require great intellectual effort, a mood of co-operation, a relaxation of some boundaries, the creation of a program that takes study of the verbal culture into the whole of the university, an assumption that humanistic study is desirable as a continuing process, a habit of mind, rather than as a skill to be mastered or a hurdle to pass over. A worse problem is that such an accomplishment would require the active participation and support of the other elements of the academic community. As my Principles imply, this is unlikely, almost against nature. Analysis of the tribes of academe themselves will help to illustrate this point. Still, one hopes that the humanists might rise to the challenge and carry their own self-interest into a debate that might be to the interest of higher education as a whole. I doubt that anyone else will.

The forms of such study will have to be worked out anew to some extent, or at least re-described, the reasons for the forms made apparent, and other faculty convinced of their importance and, in some cases, made willing to help. All of this will have to be accomplished not as an arrogation of any special authority to humanists, but as a normal exercise of their proper function. Indeed, it will require that humanists abandon the analogy with the world-hopping scientist. They must decide, as was once accepted, that every student is properly their charge, not for some course in a "basic skill," but throughout his college career. But perhaps the best appeal to humanists, as to most people, is via their own interests. If they do not reach out together to perform a more universal role, their slice of the pie will diminish further. If they act in enlightened self-interest, they will act in the best interests of higher education and society, too.

⚡ Chapter 3 ⚡

TRIBES:
LES PURS ET
LES APPLIQUÉS

BEFORE PROCEEDING with the matter of internal politics, an anthropological analysis and a differentiation of tribal (departmental) behavior is necessary. The politics of academic life are predicated on the laws of tribal interrelation, the myths of the tribes, and military history. Our analysis will involve us in a perception of various tribal units (we do not have the space or the inclination to examine all), their habits and myths, followed by a scrutiny of the division of these units into the great binary opposition between *les purs* and *les appliqués*. This will lead to a recognition of the great chaos of the tribes that is generated by the opposition, intimations of which were offered in Chapter 1.

I

Academic mythological history says that there was one original tribe of Titans responsible for the primal academic screams known as Greek and Latin. Their behavior was somewhat disorganized—we might say it was peripatetic—so in those days there was a complete and desirable absence of an administrative class. This original tribe was a great race of huge stature, from whom, it is said, we have all descended. Theirs was the Golden Age. They spoke interchangeably two tongues, in which was contained all the wisdom of the universe. There followed upon this Edenic and pastoral situation a Fall. Far back in time, and virtually forgotten by academic man today, there occurred the corruption of the race and the arrogation to themselves by some of its members of the role of a sort of priesthood. There was made of the primal tongues an arcane possession. It was the first phase of the Fall.

There followed the "Babel of tongues" phase. New barbarous languages emerged in the areas abandoned when the priesthood retreated into protecting the mysteries. The members of the original tribe, wandering in the wasteland of this babble in their accustomed peripatetic fashion, began to form enclaves in isolated caverns, and soon they established their own tongues. Enclosure astonishingly diminished their physical stature. It is claimed now that they have mixed with alien blood and have lost all knowledge of or interest in the ancient tongues, which linger on only in technical lists, corrupted traditional maledictions, and mottoes, the true meanings of which are lost. The myth that the original Titans, malingering in some deep cavern in hideous ruin and shadowy substance, will some day return is rarely uttered today.

One group, pretending to direct descent from the original priesthood, claims knowledge of the tongues. Some say that these people are impostors and cannot really speak Greek and Latin, but merely laboriously decipher the surviving texts, make lists, and teach these techniques to a few neophytes, who are initiated into the tribe annually, at the autumnal equinox, in secret and allegedly obscene rites. The decline and fall of the purest of *les purs* have been only occasionally reversed under conditions in which a leader of the old imperialistic sort invades the domains of archeology, early medieval history, and philosophy, returning with captured bands of neophytes and publishing periodic declarations of outrageous intent.

For the most part, however, those of the tribe of classicists remain relatively retiring, like the mythical malingering great race. The overwhelming of the hegemony of the classicists is complete. Even Oedipal resentment against the tribe, which lingers in the minds of some of the elderly and middle-aged, has waned appreciably. The eclipse of their professed subjects is often regretted by English professors, who now have the virtually hopeless task of teaching by crude frontal assault the proper writing of the barbarous tongue—something few students of Latin did not learn indirectly in the days of the old priesthood. However, it is more than doubtful that English professors, who belong to a tribe that broke from the priesthood relatively early, would themselves welcome a return of the old Saturnians to ease their task, which provides coin of the realm in periods of drought, famine, and invasion by barbarous tribes rather inaccurately called "social scientists." The reason for this rejection of the classicists is the fundamental Principle of Tribal Behavior which says that *guardianship of the sacred turf is regarded in every tribe as a sacred duty.*

II

The tribes of literati, among which English is the largest and most powerful, have sought on occasion to arrogate to themselves the role of the old Titanic priesthood ever since the insinuation of English literature into the old classical curriculum; but it is indeed hardly more than a role; and the English tribe, not exactly anarchic, but comprised of active subgroups often in conflict, contemplates from time to time the fate of the classic Titans, who, it is said, were unable to adjust to a faster pace, staggering as they were under the weight of an epidermis of thickly accumulated footnotes. Under the pressure of such anxiety, the trendier of the new tribesmen contemplate writing books entitled *What Was Literature?* and *The Art of Flash Gordon* and escape to the cinema and to structuralist analyses of soap operas, game shows, and sartorial fashion. These activities, developed *inside* the tribe, are unlike those external forces which nearly extinguished or at least made mortal the classicists. They seem at first glance to be more like the behavior of lemmings than tribal behavior. In most cases they are variations of the periodic march of a group of humanists into the great amorphous sea of social science. The late Professor Donald Stauffer proposed as a possible explanation of the lemmings' behavior the idea that they are unconscious Malthusians, but he abandoned the hypothesis in favor of no explanation at all. However, this leaves us unsatisfied with respect to explanations of humanists' behavior.

Why this periodic breakaway from the mass and consequent movement to the sea? The literary tribesman has always had to face the difficulty of distinguishing the fashionable from the excellent and significant. In the great amorphous sea of social science, there is seen to occur the miracle in which fashion itself becomes significant as a subject for mystification and objectification, and is then pored over. The advent in recent years of greater emphasis in the curriculum on near-contemporary literature has intensified tribal anxiety with respect to fashion. The fashion changes so rapidly that the literary scholar suspects that he is the buffoon in a French bedroom farce. Milton used periodically to be raised up and Donne sent down, then vice versa, but the process was slow, and one might witness only one complete cycle in a career. There is now more material produced every day to be raised and lowered than could have been imagined not too long ago. A tribesman of modern literature constantly suspects that his antiquity is showing.

But even more alarming is the idea that literature itself may be disappearing (a concept fostered, incidentally, on the inside of the tribe, the members of which may be the only ones to have heard of it). Antinovels, antipoems, and antiplays abound. To be sure, these turn out upon investigation to be literature after all, but the literature professor faces the more exotic fear of the disappearance of literature by expansion rather than classical contraction. When everything verbal or actable—including role-playing outside the theater—becomes literature, literature is nothing and the tribal subject is merely more grist for the mill of the social sciences, or, as William Blake put it, ". . . a web, dark & cold, throughout all / The tormented element stretched."

On top of all this, a sense of anxiety pervades the literati, for deep in their hearts lurks a suspicion that in the age of literature's possible disappearance literary study is effete, dilettantish, bourgeois, and appropriate only for modern-day counterparts of Marius the Epicurean. There rises therefore periodically in the tribe a movement to make sense of the subject by submitting it to political, psychological, historical, or other modes of analysis. Thus the march toward the sea begins anew.

It is possible that the tribe will survive in greater numbers than the old classicists because of its capacity to contain inner strife and to enlarge or contract its scope at various critical moments like some huge polypus. One such expansionist breath several decades ago took in a swarm of poets and novelists, who for a while at least provided the Heraclitean element that may be the key to all tribal health. If one asks a so-called creative writer (the epithet is much disliked) what the problem of most professors of literature is, he is likely to reply, "That's easy; they hate literature." There is just enough evidence of this in the periodic march to the sea to make the remark grounds for genuine conflict inside the tribe. This conflict is the English-department version of the great binary opposition of *les purs* and *les appliqués*, the creative writer taking the view that practice is nobler than theory or at least not leechlike, the scholar-critic convinced that the writer knows not what he does or at least turns fumbling, inarticulate, or outrageously egotistical and coy when he attempts to explain.

This kind of opposition flows through our subject. We leave it momentarily to remark that the anxieties we have mentioned, plus the experience gained in careers immersed in the study and/or practice of verbal intricacy, render many of these tribesmen particularly savage and adept in intertribal encounters and displays of wit. Oscar Wilde was the precursor not of the antiacademic aesthete (a lost species) but of the academic critic of all that comes in his morning mail, which includes the hackneyed and illiterate prose of the campus newspaper, the hackneyed and arrogant Newspeak of all campus bureaucrats, and the hackneyed and ambiguous meanderings of the college president. With such creatures, beware asking the innocent question, even in the line of duty:

"Professor X, I just don't understand this idea of case."

"Mr. Y, *you* are a case!"

The admission of the subclass of creative writers into the tribe has, some will claim, introduced an irritating but beneficial capriciousness into its very heart. Perhaps it is better to say that there has been institutionalized the role (for it is only a role) of what W. B. Yeats would have called the hunchback or fool, but given its self-consciousness is perhaps best called the fakir. Few other academic tribes have so systematized this venerable institution, which tends, when working properly, to drain tribal councils of pomposity and to require toleration of an appropriate amount of antibureaucratic posturing and irresponsibility. In Chapter 1, I offered an instance of the crafty use of this institutional role by a poet. It is an example of the Principle stated by Professor Northrop Frye that *writers are expected to bite the hand that feeds them.* The behavior that goes with this has been in the past characterized by unconventionalities in clothing, conveyance, appearance of office, and conduct toward students of opposite sex, failure to answer official correspondence, answering correspondence in insulting doggerel, eccentricity in grading, taking occasional rest cures after issuing threats of violence, and deliberate absence from tribal councils or significant silence when present.

However, in an age when literature and other arts sometimes appear to be becoming everything and therefore nothing, the faculty creative writer discovers his role to be usurped by practically everyone. His cherished differences are submerged in mass Bohemianism when everyone, if not a poet, is a potter, a recorder player, a sand sculptor, or at least a rich hippie. As a result it has recently been observed that writers have been complaining about the lack of solid scholarly training in their students, while scholars have donned boots and overalls.

III

I have already characterized social science as a great sea, mainly because so many social scientists seem to be at sea. If the tribes of literati fear that literature (and with it their discipline) is to disappear, the social scientists wonder if their discipline has ever really existed. Even before coming to the great schism between *les purs* and *les appliqués*, one faces in the anthropography of this tribe a binary opposition—not of raw and cooked, but of hard and soft. It has been recently written in the annals of a schismatic sect of this tribe that those who are hard shall become soft and those already soft shall write autobiographies. But not without guilt all around. In the behavior of the social scientists there is a curious inversion of the accepted system. Ritual arises out of mime, rather than mime out of ritual. The social scientist mimes—and therefore develops his rituals out of—the hierarchical orders of the pure sciences, with all the obeisance to power, position, and authority implicit therein. But to the observer the social scientist's face is painted and his ruff protrudeth. Opposed to the happy clownishness of the creative writer, the social scientist is the solemn tragic mime. One chairman of psychology is known to have worn cap and gown on the first visit he made to a new dean. His tenure is said to have been short, but his act expressed the requisite pathos and flamboyance, though cap and bells might have been more appropriate. Inside the tribe, the ritual requires that no one, under penalty of invective, *admit* that it is a mime, but there is much veiled recognition that it is. The tension thereby created leads annually to attempts to navigate across the sea to some promised port where all will be leis and dancing girls and where it is said to be possible to mimic a genuine poet or beach bum for years without detection. This behavior has apparently been institutionalized and no doubt even studied.

The drive toward mimicry originates in the insatiable desire continually to be hard—to mathematize, to quantify, to abstract perfectly. There are cases of guilt about not being as hard as one ought. This is the reason that the so-called science of man threatens ever to become the science of rats, then the science of matter, and finally the science of pure symbols. Certainly a Principle applicable to the tribe here is that *hardness can be sustained only so long*. There is apparently always a return or a defection, called by some a loss of mathematic nerve, by others humanism. But this does not account for the threatened engulfment of the humanists by the great sea of social science. Rather it is explained by the miraculism already mentioned—called scavenging by some—that renders everything an object of study, though an elusive object indeed.

It is not surprising that this situation results in a self-absorption that isolates the tribe from the humanists on one side and the pure scientists on the other. The result is a group of self-proclaimed pariahs who hope to be left alone so as not to be reminded that they are not hard enough.

Beyond this first opposition looms the universal one of *les purs* and *les appliqués*. This sorts the members of the tribe differently; we apprehend the four cardinal points of hard-*pur*, hard-*appliqué*, soft-*pur*, and soft-*appliqué*. The applied social scientist claims involvement, indeed shouts it at the uninvolved purist, whose theories may never achieve the revered relevance. On this side is a combination of aggressiveness and feelings of inferiority. On the other side the *purs* combine feelings of superiority and gnawing doubt. The *appliqués'* sense of inferiority stems from their relatively short history as a recognized tribe, but also from the capriciousness of the social situations with which they claim to deal. Indeed, yesterday's solution seems often to be the source of today's problem. It is said, cynically (I hope), by some inside the tribe that this is a *Good Thing*, since it always assures a set of problems with which to deal. For others, it is a source of depression. It is argued by some that *les appliqués* in this tribe are by nature impatient with pure research and even thought. The sense of superiority mustered by *les purs* is part of the mime already mentioned. The pure scientist looks down from his Brahmin heights only when he must at the world of the engineer. The social scientist creates his own lower caste in emulation.

The persistence of the social scientist on his great sea, the huge albatross of relativism draped about his neck, cannot help eliciting a certain respect from other mimers. That the study of a social situation changes it and invalidates the study's results was a discovery that first sent shock waves through the tribe, but with characteristic ingenuity this problem itself was turned into an object of study, and the social scientist thereby assured himself of an infinite regress of issues every bit as intractable as those dense medieval theological problems that kept churchmen busy for centuries. The fact that observation affects the observation is the social scientist's version of romantic irony, but it must be noticed at last that it too is a principle mimed from the pure sciences.

IV

At the edge of the tribe—of it and not of it—exists a group that claims actually to be of direct, pure descent from the founders, with members now sometimes involved in, sometimes apart from, the tribe's everyday activities. These fringe people, who have clung to the old temporal—now called "diachronic," as opposed to "synchronic"—fashion of the tribe, practice their own versions of hard and soft scholarship. The struggle inside the group called historians seems to be to establish an identity in that curious fringe area they inhabit and to find out, as one tribesman once declared to me, "what in hell we are doing." Mating dances, including vulgar displays, before computers, are known recently to have occurred, this being as hard as a historian can get; others have whispered that they must all move outward still farther from the tribal omphalos toward recognition that history is an art form, invoking the problem of their linguistic medium, making it every bit as mysterious as that of the literati. These insistent theorists, though regarded as soft, persist with a veritably gleeful sadism to attack all those who would move confidently from data to solution without worrying the question of the verbal medium they employ. It is whispered that some of these theorists have covertly been studying with the priests of the literati.

In any case, the interest in history stands as an embarrassment to *les purs* and *les appliqués* of the tribe of social scientists, both of whom seem to have abandoned the diachronic dimension at about the same time. The historians are, then, an outgroup. They express a certain pathos, even, I think, a tragic condition, in a time when their vision is sorely needed. Without the opportunity in any formal sense to be *appliqués*, they feel compelled to argue about the future on the basis of their apprehension of the past. It is not surprising that their stance sometimes appears pompous and their expression long-winded, their styles anachronistic and their gestures desperate. To read the future from the past does curiously have the character of Professor Mircea Eliade's archaic man, who in the end denies the fact of time by connecting it to cyclical return. But no matter, the brethren are not listening.

V

Among the tribes it seems to have been the pure scientists who invented the modern sense of academic hierarchy and bequeathed the idea of it in all its pomposity and solemnity—including national academies and institutes—to the social scientists. One is uncertain whether the constant comparison of departments and individuals nationwide, and the rating of everybody as in the top six of his field, is really more than a crazy game to the social scientists, but to the pure scientists it is brute reality, every bit as much as gravity was reality to Newton. The pure scientists unanimously consider the social sciences soft and themselves perpetually hard. The tribal commitment to measurement flows over into attitudes toward the grading of neophytes and into the question of who in the tribe is important and who less so. The pure scientist has apparently progressed beyond the combination of aggressiveness and a sense of inferiority that characterizes the social scientist, and knows little of the irony with which the humanist views the academic world. The result is a sort of re-achieved innocence and sense of well-being that has only recently been punctured by the unbelievable behavior of governmental agencies toward the fine scientific art of grantsmanship. The adjustment is slow and excruciating. But there is also an innocence of vocabulary: That which is not objective is subjective. Subjectivity is all right if kept in the area of *fun*. Therefore one should have an aesthetic interest. This turns out often to be aestheticism with a vengeance. A physicist may, and probably will at the first opportunity, reveal to you that he is an accomplished violinist, a poet, or a painter of landscapes. He may have built his own harpsichord. His ranking in the profession is his reality; therefore it is hard; therefore it is objective. The rest is art, and isn't it terrible that his students don't write better.

But where hierarchy reaches its apotheosis, where it becomes most real (or unreal, see footnote, p. 25), is in one of the realms of the scientific *appliqués*, the medical school. Where in the tribal councils of the fine and liberal arts the chairman is often (not always) an object of patronization for having chosen administration as an escape from thought, in the medical tribe such an interpretation had better not be uttered or even mused upon. In this most conservative of the academic tribes, history is purely mythological. There always *was* a chairman. There is divinely invested in him all totemic power. His wisdom is not to be questioned from below, and rage is the answer to words from above—if there is an above. It has been known that some chairmen have in the mythic past simply refused to be removed from authority by deans who sent everything but an eagle to eat out the recalcitrants' liver. The chairman's wisdom is illustrated by his huge bibliography, including the works of his students, which he may have read and to which he has signed his name, bestowing manna upon them as he does.

Under the tribal warfare of pure and applied may be classified the struggle of the medical school's basic scientists against contamination by the biological scientists and vice versa. These groups are natural enemies who publicly claim close friendship. Their battles stop this side of germ warfare, but their troops cannot inhabit the same laboratories and classrooms without their deans and chairmen casting spells and piercing effigies.

VI

The schism of the tribes, transcending hard and soft where it appears, expresses two different senses of the ideal nature of the academic universe. On one side, *les appliqués** feel that the university should be engaged and should constantly demonstrate its relevance to society by quite apparent involvement in the community. Research should reap benefits—a better tomato, health-care delivery, an effective transportation system. On the other side is the concept of the university as a preserve for pure thought, to which Immanuel Kant might have attributed purpose without purpose, where the effect of the institution is indirect and often unpredictable. The latter view stands for the radical independence of the scholar and researcher, who, ideally, is proceeding not because he is told that investigation is needed or that a certain solution must be produced, but because he thinks he may be on to something, the practical application of which may or may not be of concern to him.

In practice, these ideals are blurred in all the tribes known to me. *Les purs* are never as pure as they claim when they are standing on principle and *les appliqués* can in private be quite pure indeed. But in the politics of the tribes these poles remain gathering points, and there is some ground, though I resist establishing a Principle, to claim that those tribes which encompass and contain the differences retain a certain Hera-

---

* It is necessary to say here that a very patient engineering dean paid several visits to my office to attempt to convey to me the difference between a professional school and a school of applied science. I recognize the difference, and so that he may conclude that his efforts have not been entirely wasted, I have refrained from discussing the tribe of engineers. I recognize that the same distinction might be made by medical professors, but I run the risk of classifying them *appliqués* for the sake of the elegance of my binary discourse.

clitean vigor—if they can avoid serious acts of internal violence.

It would be convenient to declare that each of the tribes of
academe has certain social conventions that dominate the play
of its members. However, it would be stretching a point to
isolate the tribes in this way. Still, some differences among
them may be detected. It is perhaps a measure of the anxieties I have mentioned that the social scientists are given to
somewhat louder behavior and more exotic cocktails than
most of their colleagues, an exception being the historians,
who will drink anything offered to them but in their own
haunts are given to penuriousness. The literati take a basic attitude toward drink, consume a lot of it in its various rudimentary states, and eschew all group activity even when in
groups. On the other hand, scientists often indulge in the formal entertainment of games or performances and are likely to
experiment with punch in various flamboyant colors. They
are even given to dancing in the old-fashioned way, so that to
drop in on one of their gatherings seems to disorient one in
time. Descent into debauchery and drunkenness among the
social scientists is direct and relatively rapid; among the humanists deliberate, stately, and morose; among the scientists
in the manner (when it occurs) of the fraternity party. It
remains to be said that what the professors of medicine and
business call a party is a deductible expense.

ᨒᨒᨒ Chapter 4 ᨒᨒᨒ

RITES DE PASSAGE:
COMING OF AGE
IN ACADEME

LIFE IN ACADEME is marked by periodic rituals of ascension which bear aspects of trial by perturbation and ordeal. It has been remarked of the quest for the Ph.D. degree that the principal requisite for success is endurance of an especially saturnine character. Entrance into the better graduate schools apparently requires intelligence; initial success requires glibness and adequate preparation; but completion requires the spiritual assets of the long-distance runner. After survival to a certain point, dogged persistence or simply bovine presence will complete the ordeal. At the very end, success is nearly inevitable, since professorial advisors believe themselves at this point to be as much on trial as the candidate. Exceptions are rare. Candidates have been known on occasion to set out by car or bus for the final examination only to be heard from again in Hawaii or Alaska; and momentary incapacity has sometimes caused delay. But all in all the test of endurance creates self-selection: those continue who can run the requisite distance and whose hearts are attuned to the pace.

Earning the doctorate is a process incorporating a number

of rituals preliminary to those later *rites de passage* on which
the faculty member's academic career turns. These important
moments are little known to outsiders, who imagine the obvious solar rituals of the academic calendar (to be discussed in
Chapter 5) as basic. Nothing could be further from the truth.
While the solar rituals are annual, quaternary, and binary,
the internal rituals are stretched out along the whole career of
the professor in purely linear, rather than cyclic, form. These
rituals, or trials, take somewhat different shape in different
tribes, but bear a familial relationship of structure nevertheless. Field work that I have undertaken in this area has been
principally among the tribes of literati, and what follows
deals mostly with them. The trials I shall study are: (1) the
professional convention (trial by fire, more specifically hot
coals), which may or may not include (2) the job interview
(trial by ice), which if survived is followed by (3) the formal
visit (trial by sword and stone). After a long hiatus there may
occur (4) the review for promotion to tenure (trial by innuendo, the final phase of which is carried on *in absentia*), and
ultimately, but only for a select few, (5) the chairmanship
(trial by descent to hell, or the dark night of the soul).

Trial by Fire. As academe has grown, so have the annual
national conventions, at which the first trials of the neophytes
are played out. Chemists, physicists, historians, scholars of
the modern languages, and virtually all other academic
groups have evolved national societies, which play complex
roles in tribal affairs. Some of these conventions now draw
more than ten thousand people. Among them, that of the
Modern Language Association is one of the largest, and
around it has grown up a considerable body of legend. This
gathering of the various tribes of literati takes place, for some
unknown reason perhaps anciently connected with the winter
solstice, every December 26–30, at just the time when some
professor starting out for the site in Chicago or New York is

likely to be set down in Montreal or Atlanta to wait out a snowstorm.

The convention has outgrown any hotel of imaginable size. Mere attendance, for the neophyte, is a trial by fire. He must plan his itinerary and arrange his lodgings months in advance, or he will be relegated to camping on the very outer fringes of the enclave. When he arrives he waits in line to register for his convention name tag; he discovers himself nearly suffocated in anxious crowds waiting for elevators. He may have to walk several flights of hotel stairs to be on time for an appointment (for he is probably there to be interviewed for a job). He must wait in a long line in any reasonably nearby restaurant. His pastimes during the period of the convention are: attendance at meetings where scholarly papers are delivered to large, restless audiences (an experience that has badly burned and depressed more than a few neophytes); wandering among the exhibits of textbook producers and university presses (where it appears that everybody except *him* has a book on display); malingering in the lobby, where everyone is talking in an animated way to everyone else (but *he* is clearly alone). He notes that the manners of the tribe in this situation change remarkably from all that he has previously known. Tribesmen become Rotarian. They hurry about, looking important. They move through the lobby peering not into each other's faces but at each other's chests. Soon he adapts himself to this behavior, construing name tags and making a sport of locating in the throng scholars whose books he has read. Or he may flee to the nearest bar, where he fortifies himself for still more of the same. Returning, he suffers the depressed feeling that everyone else has some important business here, that everyone but him knows everyone else, and that he is an outsider and will probably always be condemned to such a role. So powerful is this feeling that a whole class of attendees speak even into middle age as if they did not belong there. In the evening of the first day occurs the *moment of despond,* when the neophyte considers refusal of the quest and is tempted by the allurements of a return to his vacation. If he overcomes this urge he may locate friends with whom he can trade stories over strong drink. To hear the stories is part of the ordeal, for they are about the job interview; yet often they have a strangely calming effect, the neophyte slipping gradually into the realm of experience and irony.

Trial by Ice. The reason most neophytes attend these gatherings is to pass this trial, the job interview. In fact, it has come to appear that the meetings are now held for this express purpose, their original aims being lost in prehistory. In a tight market, if the neophyte has good fortune, some departmental chairmen will have arranged interviews with him in advance. The interviewer has probably scheduled one interview per hour, morning and afternoon, and sometimes well into the evening. The neophyte must plan his physical approach with care. If he starts out from the lobby he may have to wait twenty minutes for an elevator to the interviewer's floor. If he starts out from his own room, he may discover that the elevator simply will not stop for him, and he may have to walk several flights. Therefore, it is imperative that he have trained assiduously for steep climbs. Endurance, however, should not be a problem, since each neophyte has already demonstrated it by having advanced as far as he has.

Indeed, it is the interviewer who is more likely to be suffering from fatigue. The neophyte should remember this. His own greater problem is shock: he has been struggling through hordes of people, whose behavior is in absolute contradiction to his image of the profession; he has observed the anxieties of his fellow job-hunters; he has undergone the bureaucratic difficulties of getting to a lobby telephone; he has experienced frustration in locating friends; even his own dissertation director, who has promised him introductions, seems to have disappeared. For a few neophytes there is, however, something wildly exhilarating in all of this. It is a true vision of Old Chaos, an unexpected opening of the pit. It is no surprise, therefore, that on about the second day of the convention one may observe an occasional neophyte moving about in a state of transport with burning eyes and fixed smile. The proper spell for his spouse, upon the neophyte's return is:

> *Weave a circle round him thrice,*
> *And close your eyes with holy dread.*

For the experienced convention-goer, the professor with tenure, the whole thing is, of course, merely a solar and not a linear ritual or trial. He has a nose for opportunities of which the neophyte is unlikely to be aware. One of these is the publisher's cocktail party. Attendance at these parties is ostensibly by invitation, but they seem to attract those many prowlers who sense their presence like the crackle of a twig in the forest. The publisher, who ought properly to be dressed in pith helmet and bush jacket, tolerates freeloading within limits, for there is always thought to be the chance to buy another Manhattan from the natives in the form of a popular textbook idea. These parties are held in hotel rooms or small suites and are jammed with people, some of whom have been cruising the halls, sharklike, in search of life.

There are also departmental parties, the styles of which vary. Generally they are more sedate, for they are usually designed to show off graduate students to prospective employers. They are flesh markets within what has come to be a flesh market.

When in search of new personnel, some departments do up the whole convention operation in patrician style, commandeering a suite, complete with a secretary (British accent desirable) who screens calls while the chairman interviews and senior professors drop in and out according to a discreet schedule. Other chairmen eschew such grandeur and go it alone in a single room.

The neophyte approaching his interview tends to forget that the chairman or interviewer he is about to confront is fatigued, has probably been through it all many times before, and also wishes he were elsewhere. His lack of awareness in this respect is the neophyte's last vestige of naïveté about faculty members. It is the residue of the freshman's idea that faculty members have no *real* existence and are merely essences (see p. 36). The truth is that the interviewer has probably been up late the night before at some meeting and has in any case arrived at the convention directly either from some departmental crisis or from several days of sharing the house with holiday visitors. If it is late in the day, he has already conducted several interviews and may not have escaped from his hotel room for hours. As a result he may have only an unsteady sense of who the person before him is and may fail to ask important questions, in the belief that he has already asked them; or he may ask a series of questions appropriate to the *next* scheduled interview, leaving the neophyte with the impression that he is dealing with a Thurber hero or even the Mad Hatter. There may be truth in this latter impression, since on occasion certain Mad Hatters have become chairmen. If fatigue is his condition, the interviewer will appreciate all the help he can get, and the candidate has the opportunity to turn the whole affair into an exhibition of tact and management.

But there are other sorts of encounters. One candidate reports that upon knocking on the door he heard a shuffle and a thud, the door opening to a view of the chairman supine on the floor, looking up and introducing himself. The situation was never recovered. Another tells of a double interview by a harried chairman who had fallen behind schedule and attempted to deal with two candidates at once. All that came of this was an enduring bond of friendship between the two neophytes. Others have brought back tales of massive interviews in which ten to a dozen faculty members hurl questions at the candidate, who is pressed up against a television set or sandwiched on the edge of a bed between two professors. In the midst of all such trials the phone rings periodically, interrupting one's best accounts of one's dissertation or how one would teach *The Tempest* to sophomores. Returning from a call, the interviewer may only vaguely remember to whom he is talking or about what, leaving the candidate in midsentence wondering whether he should continue over what now looms as slippery and barren terrain.

Trial by Sword and Stone. Successful passage of trial by ice means that the candidate emerges from the tundra to visit the academic institution that has now shown serious interest in him. Nevertheless, in spite of this good sign, the campus may turn out to be a castle perilous. It is not that the candidate will be expected to draw the sword from the stone, though devious questioning by some senior professors may require some tugging. Rather, the candidate must employ his only real weapon of defense, that sword in his mouth, both to ward off and to score palpable hits. At this stage a new element enters the situation, because having decided after debate to spend some of its meager funds to bring this particular candidate to trial, the department finds itself in an ambivalent role. It hopes the candidate will sell himself, and it tries to sell itself, though sometimes very ineptly. Thus the elder tribesmen don garish masks of good humor and well-being and appear to ingratiate themselves, in a spirit that sometimes approaches jocularity. The candidate is offered drink. He is returned to his hotel late. And then he is informed that during the whole of the next day he must run a gauntlet, from administrative officers who in a spirit of great magnanimity offer to respond to any thrust he attempts, past young faculty who proudly and sometimes sullenly display their wounds, to a group of selected students, armed with stones, who will want to know how he relates to the in-groups, the out-groups, and the issues of the day. He will describe his doc-

toral dissertation perhaps a dozen times during his visit, formulating his description, perfecting it, then varying it
through boredom, and finally concluding to himself that the
whole thing was a mistake and he himself is a tendentious ass.
The candidate may, the next day, give a lecture, during
which a professor emeritus may fall asleep in the front row
and an assistant professor scowl with contempt in the back.
Questions following it will be delivered in the swashbuckling
manner of the late Errol Flynn by those who do not let an opportunity for swordplay with a lesser go by. The questioners
will be assistant professors preparing for the rite of promotion
and trying to make themselves better known to their elders,
who (they suspect) do not remember their names or have
them confused with someone else. However, such questions
are usually blunt and without poisoned tips, unlike those that
may be delivered in comparative solitude and with deceptive
good nature by senior faculty. These veterans' tongues are
whetted to a fine edge, and they are particularly contemptu-
ous of gauche lunges. They expect swordplay complete with
deference to and appreciation of their own moves. To engage
in the trial with real *sprezzatúra* is dangerous. But controlled
exuberance is allowable and often impressive.

The upshot of the visit is either an offer of acceptance into
the tribe or a vaguely worded series of sad and friendly utterances, which translated say, "Thou shalt not pass." Yet acceptance into the tribe by no means indicates immediate admission to the tribal councils, for that requires successful
endurance of

Trial by Innuendo. This ordeal begins with the moment of
appointment to an untenured position and lasts until tenure is
granted or one's contract is not renewed. Usually, tenure and
an associate professorship are granted at the same time, but
more and more often these days tenure is being withheld even
at the associate level. The uncertainty can continue as long as

seven years. In the end the decision rests principally with the already tenured faculty of one's department, arguing the case in the absence of the candidate. The traditions that enfold this act of judgment differ somewhat from tribe to tribe. There are those that favor the secret, and those that favor the open ballot. In some departments, more than a simple majority is required. Behind the complexities of voting lie the conventions of power. Subchiefs of the tribe exert an unquantifiable authority. In the sciences, the leader of the candidate's research group is usually able to dictate the outcome by virtue of the convention of *noblesse obliqe* and of the specialized nature of the group's research, which means that few tribesmen outside the group feel themselves qualified to make an independent judgment. Besides, in taking this position, they escape responsibility. Then, too, they are aware of the greater workability of a group in which the subchief is at ease with his troops. In other fields, something of the same applies, though the subgroupings are never so formalized and hermetically sealed. Still, the senior eighteenth-century scholar in English is not likely to be frustrated in his desire either to promote or to terminate a young colleague in his field. But probably not without extensive debate, which may range far away from the qualifications of the candidate to questions of where the department is heading, where the discipline is heading, and how everything got into the state it is in.

No matter which situation exists, the untenured assistant professor suffers progressively more acute torment. At the outset, the year of decision seems remote. Flushed with success at having passed the earlier trials, and surrounded by neophytes of his own, he is busy and involved. But trial by innuendo is also trial by tightening of the vise. The candidate's behavior inevitably changes. Those tribesmen who first greeted him with colorful grinning masks now seem to hop about him in attitudes of ruthless ominousness. Each year he learns by attention to the considerable mythology of the untenured that so-and-so was let go because he offended so-and-so, defeated him in tennis, lost to him in tennis, did not play tennis, was heard to criticize his tennis or tennis as such. As time passes, the assistant professor begins to sharpen his defenses by formulating whispered or silent criticisms of his elders, their scholarship and research, and their judgment, in preparation for the day when they may find him wanting and he needs such excuses. In the mythology of the untenured it is said that candidates have lost tenure because of the departmental secretary's prejudice against them, because a spouse has become unruly or not unruly, because students have actually liked them, or, of course, because of politics. It seems universally to be asserted that judgments are capricious. Therefore, some—cracking under the strain—set out to ingratiate themselves by losing or winning at tennis, organizing the softball team, or developing a reputation for willingness to do odd jobs of no matter what menial sort around the department.

In fact, it has not been conclusively shown that any of these moves is effective, though a good shortstop is rarely known to have been fired anywhere. However, taking on the role of odd-jobber can often end in disaster for the candidate if the case is marginal in other respects. A willing worker is one thing, but a menial one brings out all of the faculty's latent elitism.

At the major universities in this country, where most of the research in academe is carried on, the three announced criteria for promotion are usually research, teaching, and university service. About the first two I shall have more to say at the end of this chapter, when I take up the political issues that this most crucial rite of passage raises. With respect to judgment on the basis of these criteria the tribes form a spectrum from the strict quantifiers to the nonquantifiers. At the quantifying extreme, promotion to tenure requires a certain *amount* of publication. It is said in the mythology of the un-

tenured that this amount can be precisely gauged: so many
articles equals a book; a textbook counts so much; and so
forth. No extreme of this sort is personally known to me,
though I have met professors who have invoked purely quan-
titative personal judgments. There may actually be whole
tribes using such systems. The nonquantifying ebbs out at
the other extreme into claims for the excellent nonpublishing
teacher. It is interesting to observe how in the mythology of
the untenured the unpublished candidate for tenure is
frequently declared an excellent teacher, the spectrum of
frequency of publication often being turned into a binary opposition between the apparently exclusive virtues of research
and of teaching, when evidence of research is lacking, and
thence into a moral judgment between evil and good. Spectrum and opposition vary among the tribes, depending on the
nature of the institution, with some liberal-arts colleges practicing the admirable principle of teach or perish, and most
major universities adhering to an appropriate publish-or-
perish principle. Those more or less in the middle, and some
at either end, give a sort of lip service to both teaching and
publishing, without defining a system of judgment that es-
tablishes any standard except that of rumor.

The drive toward sheer quantification is the result of a
number of things: the naïve assumption that such quantification really brings truth, the desire for bureaucratic simplicity, the relief that quantification brings to those who may
now avoid real judgment. As a result of these conveniences
there have been efforts to quantify teaching effectiveness as
well as research. Bizarre point systems based on student polls
have been devised. A department I have heard of developed
one with grading on a scale of 1 to 100. In practice, everyone
was rated within a spread of ten points. This department,
which had made much public noise over the importance of
teaching, had thereby satisfied itself about the competence of
its own members, but in doing so had in fact very nearly re-

moved teaching ability from the criteria for promotion. The system, I am told, was pressed by young faculty. It is interesting that the group contained a large number in the unionization movement.

The effectiveness of the trial of promotion depends on the traditions of the tribe and the quality of the tenured faculty who have come up through it. Different systems, of course, yield different types of faculty. In the mythology of the untenured, as I have suggested, the tenured faculty members seem to become more ominous as the day of judgment looms closer. It is imagined that certain of them are in a lather of prejudice and resentment against youth, brilliance, and originality. In my experience, something quite different usually occurs. I know of cases where prejudice and personal dislike ruled, but they are fewer than imagined and are for the most part limited to tribal situations that have had a tradition of corruption. Generally, if there is ferociousness it is attributable to discomfort at having to decide against someone. To deny tenure, it is often forgotten, is usually to admit error in the hiring process. This must be covered over by lamentations on the theme of arrested development. Tribal councils engage in elaborate evasive tactics before they bring themselves to a hard, negative decision. Most faculty members are by nature not very anxious to perform such a task, and many will go to considerable lengths if not to avoid it, at least to put it off. One of the problems the chairman has is to bring to a close what amounts to an unconscious filibuster against the act of termination. This leads to the Principle that *there is a ritual necessity of debate*, talk being part of the process by which guilt is assuaged. In this debate, various means by which the candidate could be given further trial are proposed, and the chairman must reiterate the rules of the tribe and hasten all to decision.

One of the criticisms frequently made of council judgment is that though it successfully weeds out real incompetence, it is also likely to terminate quirky brilliance. It is certainly possible for such errors to occur, but they are not nearly as frequent as is alleged in the mythology of the untenured, who have an exaggerated opinion of the worth of their untenured colleagues, just as the tribal councilors tend to underrate each other. The reason there are fewer errors than alleged is that quirky brilliance is extremely rare.

The main cause of error is the failure of a certain number of elders to pay any attention. With respect to teaching, I am referring not merely to the candidate's ranking in student polls, but to the many unquantifiable hints available to a professor about his colleagues' work. Professors are largely self-absorbed and sometimes sink into isolation. When it comes time to reach decisions, they can be out of it. Thus it is with considerable justification that untenured faculty are anxious about becoming known. A department that does not institutionalize ways this can be achieved risks unruly displays and occasional retribution. A Principle here is that *little will be done unless it is institutionalized, good intentions to the contrary notwithstanding.* There should be systematic ways to allow debate to occur. This is, of course, more easily advocated than brought about, since such meetings themselves can lead to misunderstandings unless an aura of good humor is cultivated. Furthermore, graduate students of any tribe have their own mythmaking tendency, and it is of a primitive sort, given to descriptions of dragon fights. They turn debate or even chance remarks into alleged hatreds and doctrinal schisms. Thus their own insecurities are fed and their own possible failures explained as "victimage." Nothing occurs by chance or play in this world of myth, and everything has ominous meaning.

Following the council of elders comes the conveyance of the news—the chairman's happy or melancholy task. Then occurs the wait for higher administrative action, which is often interpreted to be a period in which a demonic effort to find budgetary reasons to deny promotion takes place. The explanation for such behavior is general: administration is bestial and omnivorous.

If the departmental decision is favorable the now tenured faculty member notes the reappearance of masks, this time grinning with benevolence. A brief period of elation and gratification ensues. The candidate expects induction into the mysteries. But there are few mysteries, or if they exist, the really important ones seem to be in the keeping of a very few senior professors of national reputation, who are suspected of engineering all major departmental decisions and who are alleged to act behind a curtain penetrated only by the chairman searching for instruction. Further, the masks are soon put away, the associate professor discovering himself now forever separated from the perverse pleasures of the mythology of the untenured and apparently initiated into a tribal council that has no community. The shock of this discovery eases in time as the faculty member learns that he must not find but make his role. He then sets to work carving and painting a suitable array of masks. There are, of course, many roles (shaman, monk, organizer, guru, orator, entrepreneur, to name a few). Conscious choice and unconscious inclination enter here. The role of chairman is another matter and will be taken up shortly.

But should the candidate fail the test of promotion, he must still put in the rest of the academic year and possibly another before leaving the tribe. He is, though present, already a pariah. First, he is visited individually by a few elders wearing severe masks of sad friendship, occasionally indulging in verbal acts designed to purge guilt. A vague implication is left that *they* had supported the unfortunate victim but to no avail, that the whole process is irrational, and that they may be of some help in the future. Occasionally responsibility for the harsh decision is placed upon the dean. Shortly, however, these masks too are put aside, and the pariah imagines himself as having lost substance. He is unseen in the halls, an ectoplasm floating into the office to obtain his mail. The situation is exacerbated by his adoption of a slinking demeanor and absenting himself from meetings. His social life changes, and he declines invitations, even to official functions. His absence at the spring picnic goes unnoticed. Only the departmental secretary, who has developed various occult powers, has a clear sense of his existence, and she is the last to see him before he disappears entirely.

Yet the pariah does not always go quietly and by degrees, though it is devoutly to be wished that he do so. Though he is at best but insubstantial, there is the phenomenon known as the poltergeist, which after the decision knocks vigorously on the reputations of the elders with accusations of bias (often political), dislodges and hurls bricks, or makes rumbling noises in the student body about the penalization of good teaching in favor of research and about how students should have control over their own lives, which translated means that he should have full control over his. These mysterious noises are met, when possible, with silence among the elders, who hope that they will cease in time, which they usually do, though in recent years on occasion only after tiresome investigation in the manner of the Society for Psychical Research. Certain pariahs have been known to go into the desert of student rumor and activism, returning with a band of ragged followers to storm the tribal enclave. These raids are flamboyant, having some of the qualities of a Renaissance fair, and brief. A pariah who takes this route is from that point likely to be truly untouchable. Tribal drums have sent the word forth.

To carry hither and yon all news, good and bad, in all the situations I have mentioned is the chore of the chairman, who has submitted, in accepting his post, to

Trial by Descent to Hell, or the Dark Night of the Soul. The trial is not in the getting there but in the being there. Academic life is for the most part peopled by those whose talents for scholarship and ambitions in some research field are paramount. Therefore, it is likely that what seems to an outsider a promotion to an administrative post may be viewed in academe, and even by the recipient, as condemnation to ordeal or imprisonment. Even if this is not the attitude, the ritual expression of it is obligatory.

The fact is that quite a few academics have administrative talent, for scholarship and such skill are not necessarily antithetical qualities. But of all professional people, the scholar in a major university has probably the greatest degree of personal freedom to organize his day, month, and year. He is paid not for his time, but for his accomplishments. If he has become reasonably distinguished as teacher or researcher or both, he has probably put in long hours and intense effort. If the spirit moves him often, he nevertheless likes it to be the *spirit* that moves him. The administrator, on the other hand, must adhere to a rigorous schedule imposed by the conventions of the job. This is regarded by academics as supremely undesirable, definitely barbaric, and lacking in the proper *élan*. The chairmanship is perhaps a necessary evil, but offices at the level of the deanship and above are anathema. The chairman attends meetings in which must be endured the despised rhetoric of the administrative mind, regarded as similar in structure to that of a shark. The chairman deals with a budget and traffics with the dean. These are equally offensive objects. The budget, the professor declares, is not his business and is positively irrelevant to his concerns. In holding this view, he maintains the freedom to make irresponsible demands. The dean is a creature with large teeth and a paucity of thought, who is suspected of actually enjoying his work, having been acclimated to darkness in a previous chairmanship and now owl-like in the light. The professor sympathizes with his chairman, who must periodically report chillingly the horrors of deanly behavior. The chairman worries about courtesy of reception when the dean visits the tribal council, but often the tribesmen at this point don masks of sycophancy.

Although some faculty members would like to be chairmen, few if any will admit it. Therefore, the choosing of a chairman is preceded by a noncampaign in which caucuses among those who are not not running occur. If anything, this convention of silence magnifies political activity, which involves the department's wanting to reach consensus before the dean dictates a choice. There have been cases where this has had to occur, a department finding no one in its ranks acceptable to even a strong minority. On rare occasions, disarray has required the imposition of a trusted lieutenant from another department to keep order in an interim period of search outside the institution—a last resort.

To the role of chairman the Principles enumerated in Chapter 1 apply. His authority is well circumscribed, and what he achieves he does principally by listening and cajoling. One of his main tasks is to keep those who are entitled to it full of information. This may appear to be an impossible ideal, but it is in fact the most practical method of indirect cajolery. I have mentioned already (in Chapter 1) the worm's-eye view of human nature that comes with the realization that humanists are not particularly humanistic, scientists not particularly scientific, and social scientists not particularly social in their political roles. There are the dark days when the chairman will actually utter to his secretary or even to his dean the cry that he is surrounded by villains. In the past, he has usually meant his faculty, but in recent years, with increased student participation in departmental affairs, he may include selected students in his range of invective.

Meditation on the chairman's concerns suggests a lugubrious Principle that reads as follows: *The areas of political activity in which the chairman is most deeply and stressfully engaged are those in which he has the least authority.* In brief, these are three: appointments to the faculty, promotions, and curriculum. Where the chairman most makes his presence felt, if not known, is in exercising the fine art of *keeping things going*. He is, then, like the host of a perpetual talk show.* This is surely a system of bondage and frustration, particularly when the chairman finds himself defending decisions by the tribe that are not clear to him.

It is no wonder that so many successful chairmen retreat into faculty ranks at the first graceful opportunity, with vows never to let *that* happen again and deaf to suggestions that they become deans or vice-presidents. In many ways it is unfortunate for academic life that this retreat occurs. I shall have more to say about this in Chapter 7, where I shall practice the art of bureaucriticism.

Among the tribes and within them the rites of passage I have discussed raise two perennial issues for debate, and no work on the politics of academic life would be complete without mention of them, though arguments on all sides have by now suffered endless and dreary variation. These are the great questions of tenure and of the value of teaching as opposed to research. Most concepts of tenure are the result of institutionalized rumor. Tenure legally does not assure a faculty member of a job. He may be dismissed for any number of reasons as long as they are not connected with matters of intellectual freedom. This is not the place to attempt to draw legal distinctions. The point is that tenured faculty are, in fact, rarely dismissed in major institutions except under the gravest circumstances, and incompetence in the classroom is not one of these. Discussions of tenure rise to new pitches

* I discover again that I am discussing, as in Chapter 1, the situation in the so-called major institution, and I am tempted to establish the Principle that the chairman's administrative power is in inverse proportion to the prestige of the institution. Field workers submit stories of academic despotism in the lesser tribes. This despotism is accompanied by equally despotic behavior from governing boards and the like. Thus the chairman's role that I have described seems to be that in the best-possible academic world.

during periods of budgetary difficulty, when high-level administrators are suspected of thoughts of weeding out the faculty for "budgetary reasons." And tenure during this period may be attacked by young teachers without it who see themselves denied it because all the positions in the upper echelons are filled. No one disputes that tenure has values and defects, but the arguments that surge about it are often corrupted by questionable motives.

The tendency to oppose teaching to research is also a byproduct of various group anxieties. One habitual approach is to discuss the problem as if it were or ought to be the same in every kind of institution. Those who perhaps rightly claim that the drive to produce research—to publish so as not to perish—generally enhances the quality of teaching are hard pressed to demonstrate this. And those who claim the opposite can always point to serious abuses. But it seems apparent that different types of institutions ought to have different attitudes in this matter. No doubt there is an excellent sort of teaching that can arise where research and original scholarship are paramount. Some faculty members can only thrive under these conditions. Those who do not should, if they realize this, by all means get out. They will suffer nothing but anxiety and depression. But surely it has been shown that excellent teaching can be achieved where research does not go on, or goes on without much intensity. Numerous institutions in the country have had splendid reputations for providing higher education, through the M.A., without producing very much scholarship. The question of which is best is a foolish one. What we can say is that they are different and appropriate to different kinds of faculty members and different kinds of students. The main problem of any faculty is to maintain its conscientious commitment to the ideals appropriate to its particular institutional situation.

〰〰 Chapter 5 〰〰

THE RHYTHM
OF THE YEAR:
SOLAR RITUALS

WHEN JAMES THURBER'S BOTANY TEACHER returned from summer vacation, he was, as Thurber says, brown as a berry and ready again to explain plant structure to his classes. Thurber does not explicitly indicate that the professor was ready again to face Thurber, who had failed the course the previous year. Summer renewal in academic life implies a new crop of students annually. Nevertheless, the professor probably was ready to cope with this relatively slight wobble in the cyclical round, tuned as he was to the solar rhythm with a fineness unique to his profession. The solar cycle of academic life balances the linear progression of the academic career. If the *rites de passage* studied in Chapter 4 are laid out linearly to mark the movement of the heroic individual quester, the solar rituals establish the solidarity of the tribes.

Two fundamental solar patterns are discernible—the quaternary, or quarter system, and the binary, or semester system. The former divides the academic year into three parts and a summer session; the latter, into two parts and a summer session. In every tribe, periodic movements arise urging abandonment of the current system in favor of the one not in use. Like our system of weeks and months, neither perfectly fits the phenomena it is supposed to measure. Each has its defects, which become the subject of debate. Periodically, tribesmen rise to enunciate them. Those against the quarter system claim its divisions to be too short, too intense, and responsible for increased bureaucratic annoyance by virtue of the additional registration period required. Those who defend it point out that half again as many courses are offered, boredom does not as easily set in, and the system jibes with the traditional vacation periods. Indeed, the deficiency of the semester system in this respect has been acknowledged on all sides. For many years, in most institutions where it was employed, the first semester dragged to a lugubrious close only *after* the intervening Christmas recess, which was spent by students in woeful anticipation of papers due and examinations yet to be taken. Return to the campus occurred at the nadir of the year, early-morning classes beginning and late-afternoon ones ending in darkness. The quarter system dispensed with this offense against pattern and wrapped up the fall quarter before Christmas in appropriate wassail. Recently many institutions on the semester system have pushed the beginning of the academic year to early September or even late August in order to make things work out, classes ending early in May. Whether this shift has caused disruptions in life style and the baseball season I have not inquired. Certain institutions have been known to move from one system to the other and then back, a curious phenomenon being that the merits of the two systems were less the issue with many faculty members than the undesirability of change. It is said that in one case many of the same people who had resisted the quarter system years before resisted the semester system later on.

In the next few pages I intend to examine the solar cycle, using the quarter-system model. (Those familiar with the semester system can easily transpose.) Consequently I shall treat the academic year as divided into three parts: the fall quarter, or hope; the winter quarter, or endurance; and the spring quarter, or anticipation. Everything turns according to this rhythm. Its influence cannot be overestimated.

Hope. In Chapter 1, I offered a corollary to one of the Principles, which says that nothing should be done in May that can be put off to October. This is because in the fall of the year the energy level is extremely high and the strife of spring has been dissipated in the release that summer provides. Thurber's returning professor was not alone in his enthusiasm. Professors who have avoided each other in the halls from March through June now greet each other warmly in the mail room. They have, in the interim, traveled to England and consulted libraries, gotten away to the north woods, fished in Montana, acted in Stratford, San Diego, or Ashland, finished up a piece of research in their lab, done field work in Yucatan, lectured in Japan or Sligo. Even to teach in the summer session is to experience a change of pace: the students are a different mixture, the term is shorter, and the campus devoid for the most part of the *great issues*, whatever they may have been or will be. As September fades, the campus fills up suddenly again and yet is not quite so plastered with posters as in the spring, or as scrawled upon with graffiti, or as littered with refuse. Faculty members return with new plans for courses, curiosity about new staff members, and optimism about the intellectual level of new graduate seminars. The fall quarter is a period early in which deans and chairmen are able to secure from faculty members commitments to do things later in the year that would be impossible to get in February. Official rituals abound. Administrators ritually greet new students with the clichés of the moment in convocations, but the fundamental events are the president's faculty reception, the dean's faculty reception, and the chairman's faculty reception. In the rare institutions where all three occur, it is a good idea for the chairman to get his in first, for the other two can threaten the accumulation of good will stored up in the summer harvest.

The president's reception is usually billed as being for new faculty and is inevitably large and abstract. New faculty run the gauntlet of an administrative reception line, composed of people they may never see again. The chance actually to meet the president face to face may be incentive enough to attend. The food and drink will certainly not be. There will be an insipid and not insidious punch and such cookies and hors d'oeuvres as the campus caterers can cook up. Chairmen and deans are captives to the affair, and a few loyalists among the old guard will show up out of sympathy. They will huddle together, by discipline or by committee, and depart after a decent interval. Some faculty will declare the reception to have been profoundly depressing, but if the president does not go through with it, he and his spouse will be severely criticized, particularly at the women's club. Consequently the president and his spouse will both declare any reception they give to be a success, and when it is over, may even say to each other that it was a good thing that they went through with it. To some extent, not yet studied, faculty divide on the merits of such an event. One senses that those from the medical school, business school, engineering school, and agricultural school attend out of pleasure, a sense of duty, a kind of mindless obeisance to ritual, or all of these, while the social scientists approve of and dislike it and the humanists disapprove of and dislike it. The fine-arts people are not known to attend and may not have heard about it or may not have visited the campus yet, except by some crazy chance. A few spouses of new faculty will not attend, and of these a few will never attend any such event. The variety of excuses offered will be small and express a poverty of imagination. The real reasons—shyness, egocentricity, competition with the spouse, determination to do one's thing—are not acknowl-edged.

Both the president's and the dean's reception have a uni-form quality from institution to institution. One might imag-ine that the dean's reception would be socially more homoge-nous than the president's, but in reality it is not, because at the less abstract level of the college or school, the real dif-ferences, competitions, and envies reveal themselves. Thus, though the president's reception is dull in its abstractness, the dean's reception can be downright unpleasant in the conversa-tions that must be carried out. An intertribal event, it can lead to irritations involving suspicions of aggrandizement and shifts in power balance.

The chairman's reception varies greatly from tribe to tribe and according to regional custom—from the dressy, discreet, and sweaty garden party to the all-night bum fight and beer bust. The median is the preprandial cocktail party. Though introduction of new members sometimes leads to a certain stiffness, there has been known to occur the initiatory drink-ing competition. On the whole, a rule of thumb is that the larger the department, the greater the decorum, though what happens in the hours that follow adjournment is not well known. As the first event of a long season it is a good indica-tion of which spouses will go the route. Variations revolving around the Midwestern basement rec room, the southern Cal-ifornia swimming pool, and the Texas barbecue, are worthy of mention.

It is in the quarter of hope that one finds the most planning of public lectures, the optimistic development of next year's budget, and the launching forth of the campus newspaper, vowing with a large staff to improve on the quality of the previous year. For a while this improvement seems to materi-alize; then midterm exams bring defections, and preparation for finals brings pleas for aid. It is in the quarter of hope that the cycle of promotions begins, and also the search for new faculty for the following year. The former generates the first tribal tension of the season, but the latter, in its early stages, is acted out in a spirit of optimism, in fact a sky's-the-limit atmosphere. Perhaps the communal state of mind of the fall, with its crisp weather and renewal of energy, accounts for the tremendous popularity of football compared to the other college sports, or is it the other way around? In any case, early fall brings optimistic reports of a possibly successful season led by a preseason all-American.

As the quarter ends there is a lessening of enthusiasm, though despair has not set in. The budget is prepared, and there is hope. The promotions have not yet been acted upon. The faculty search has not yet been completed. The football season has not been the success trumpeted in the early blurbs, and the preseason all-American has injured a knee in midseason. Further defections from the newspaper staff have shrunk the paper's size, but it is coming out regularly nevertheless. It has not yet fixed upon an issue with which to lambaste the faculty. All this is not bad, and the Christmas vacation looms ahead with its promise of relief from the burden of classes. The Christmas party in the Administration building is without unpleasant incident.

Endurance. The year's midnight is a period of waiting in darkness. In the administration of state universities it is one of tension devoted to legislature-watching and perhaps legislature-manipulating. The quarter begins energetically enough, but without the spirit of the fall. Most action of the period is manufactured rather than spontaneous. Chairmen return from conventions with the names of candidates for positions. Certain faculty members attract offers from competing institutions. Certain graduate students have no prospects for jobs, and advisors must telephone frantically to seek new opportunities for them. The working out of these matters occupies perhaps two months, perhaps more. It develops that the department's first choices for appointment have taken other jobs. It may develop in the course of negotiations that the second choices in the meantime have flown. Meetings occur in which the situation is rethought. A ritual discussion takes place in which it is agreed that the first and second choices may have been mistakes anyway, and reconsideration makes candidates X and Y, perhaps with other research interests, suddenly more desirable. Thus departmental self-esteem is recaptured. Candidates X and Y undergo trial by sword and stone. Parties are laid on at which certain colleagues drink too much. It is raining or snowing.

The professors offered positions elsewhere closet with their friends and others whom they wish to impress, worrying out at length the implications for their careers of a move, and reaping maximum pleasure from the attention and notoriety this gives them. Yet they are in a state of anxiety about whether their colleagues and their institution will declare undying affection by recommending a raise competitive with the outside offer. Some time during this period the chairman wishes to himself that his colleague would simply take the offer and go away. Knowing he is being hustled, nevertheless he visits the dean, and argues the case for a raise all the way along the administrative line, sometimes twice if a review committee is reluctant or does not understand the professor's research. He knows that he will have to engage in the dreary task of seeking a replacement if he fails. (It is to be noted that the task of recruiting in February is viewed differently from the same task in October.) Flushed with the glow of being wanted, the professor does not wonder to what extent ennui and desire for relief have figured in the recommendation of his colleagues.

Some time during the quarter of endurance, committees at all levels of the institution struggle to find a time to meet, to define the issues, and to make sense. Their preliminary reports are or are not made. Those that are made are debated, amended, tabled, returned for further study, sent to another committee, or on rare occasions adopted (though usually at a later date). They have to do with a change in the grading system, establishment of uniform policies on when classes may be dropped, affirmation of academic freedom, a change to the semester system, evaluation of teaching, complaint about the personnel office, complaint about the purchasing office, complaint about the police department, and review of student participation in faculty governance.

It is during this period, the evenings slowly getting longer, that the student newspaper finds an issue, perhaps one of those just described, or in a calm year an action of the dean of students. The issue may, of course, go beyond campus concerns, but the administration or faculty is nevertheless likely to be held in some vague way accountable. Also, old issues from bygone years may be raised again simply to see if there is any life left in them. On some campuses these rise and fall like the turning of a prayer wheel. Meanwhile the campus paper contains less print, less news, and more harangues, and the staff has again diminished. An office coup may have thrown out the editor.

It is conceivable that the winter quarter will ebb out in mild protests. Weather can be a determining factor, even in California, where a moderate rainstorm snarls traffic, floods streets, and drives people to crisis behavior. A few professors conveniently spend two weeks lecturing elsewhere, or at brief conferences in sunnier climates. The basketball season comes to a close in disinterest. The last recruit visits the campus, the last official recruiting party occurs, and offers are made and accepted. No one is wildly pleased or disappointed; there is relief. The chairman will give no more parties until fall. His wife turns thankfully to thoughts of her garden, knowing that she must endure only the spring picnic before renewal.

If there are administrative resignations they frequently

occur toward the end of the quarter of endurance, that last
darkness preceding the return of light.

Anticipation. But there is an ambiguity about the light.
Legislature-watching turns into governor-watching as the
budget proceeds through channels. Hope dims as cherished
capital-improvement plans are blue-penciled and it becomes
clear that the budget probably will not contain acknowl-
edgment of inflation. Yet the spring recess brings release,
sometimes in a bursting forth that causes mass arrests in
towns along the southern coasts. The campus newspaper,
now reduced to a staff of die-hards, including perhaps a few
fanatics, concerns itself mainly with a savage attack on student apathy and on a faculty body that seems to have frustrated the year's favorite reform.

The spring riot is so well publicized that it requires little
comment here beyond the observation that it is likely to occur
in some form, whether or not there is a good political motiva-
tion. This is not to say that the famous Cambodia rebellion of
1970 was merely a variation of the spring riot. It did, however, absorb the conventions of the spring riot, and made a
separate one a needless redundancy. The spring riot is a free-
form ritual. Attempts to institutionalize it have on occasion
been successful, but for the most part have resulted in separate events. In periods of stress the Princeton house-party
weekend does not eliminate the occasional spontaneous trash-
ing of Nassau Street. Nor did the taming of the notorious
"cane spree" at the same institution. Nor does the picnic day
at Davis necessarily eliminate marches on the chancellor's office.

These are all student events. Faculty members occasionally
participate in or even foment them, but generally they turn
inward to construct their own private riots, including on occasion shedding a spouse, going native, or seeking a rest cure.
Official social life, after the pressure of winter and the many

committee meetings whose deliberations are coming to an un-
satisfactory end, lags and then nearly collapses entirely.
Chairmen, having completed the recruitment season, seek the
solace of the study. It is more difficult to find anyone in his
office. Annoyances which had been forgotten or laid aside in
the fall blossom in the cruel month of April, and professors
find themselves avoiding certain nemeses in the academic
body politic. The pariahs among the assistant professors slink
through the halls, almost invisible symbols of communal
guilt. The veteran faculty member's social life contracts to a
round of close friends with whom he can still bear to discuss
local matters. Certain of the faculty deliberately, as a result of
past experience, cease reading the campus paper, which is
about to exceed its budget and shrinks in both size and verbal
competence, though expansively shrill till the end. The departmental spring gathering is perhaps more successful if
planned as a picnic rather than a cocktail party, mere recrea-
tion in the former being less likely to exacerbate frayed
nerves. At a picnic, the presence of children provides a useful distraction, if they have not yet reached late adolescence.

One is uncertain whether the anticipation of summer, all
passion spent, does not actually shorten tempers and make
spring progress in political matters more difficult. One
guesses that fine attunement to the solar rhythm may induce
everyone to play quite naturally the emotional roles of the
seasons.

Yet the spring quarter can have its recompenses, for man
lives on anticipation. Further, there are escapes into tennis,
golf, and softball. The college baseball season, so dramat-
ically opposed in pace to the sport of the fall, ebbs out with
almost no one having known it began. But at quarter's end
there is an upbeat. Faculty members are again for a moment
seen speaking to one another, exchanging summer plans, and
the chairman has even managed to detect enthusiasm and
hope born anew as the schedule of classes for fall opening

(that distant event) is completed and professors anticipate new and better course plans and lively topics. After commencement, it is said that even the president smiled with relief as he was helped out of his cap and gown. The senior with the duck on his head and the young woman with the goat didn't ruffle him a bit when they came through the line, and the protest posters at the rear were blocked in part from view. In any case, he had simply taken off his glasses, and what the posters said merely blurred inconsequentially into the crowd.

Sabbatical Cycle. The seven-year phenomenon known as the sabbatical leave requires mention, since it provides a measure by which some faculty regard their own careers. Sabbaticals are periods for scholarship and research away from teaching. The classic sabbatical is a year abroad fortified with support from a foundation or the government. Faculty members will go to great trouble and endure almost any hardship to experience the sabbatical in full. This includes the wholesale uprooting of the family, complete with a new language and school situation for the children and a return to primitivism in the cooking arrangements for wives unfortunate enough to have to serve, though many are intrepid. The sabbatical often involves the renting of the house, but this is easy enough, since new young faculty are desperate for housing, and some professors are suspected of making a career of living in the houses of professors on leave.

The main result of the sabbatical may be the professor's developing definite Anglophile, Francophile, or like characteristics, complete with accent and wardrobe. No doubt he has joined for the year a small enclave of other scholars wherever he is researching. He may return an expert on the country he has visited and give lectures. They may be bad, they may be good. One never knows. He becomes a critic of the theater and perhaps of music, and he discourses at will on the Common Market or North Sea oil. Toward the two-thirds mark of the sabbatical year he will have wondered idly about how things were going at home, and in the end he will be happy to return, prepared again to teach whatever it is he teaches to his classes.

⚬⚬⚬⟶ *Chapter 6* ⟵⚬⚬⚬

STYLES AND
THE DECAY OF STYLE

Scene: *The fall-quarter academic convocation, a balcony of the library overlooking the procession route.*

Characters: CYRIL *and* VIVIAN, *faculty members not participating.*

CYRIL [*on the balcony*]: My dear Vivian, don't coop yourself up hours on end in the library. It is a lovely morning and the convocation procession is beginning. Come out and enjoy the nostalgic gowns, the colorful hoods, and mortarboards. It is rare today to see the true academic style on display.

VIVIAN [*ambling through the French doors, a fanfare signaling the procession heard in the distance*]: I have come out, but not to observe the academic style, which seems to me hardly to exist and perhaps never to have existed. Those who believe it did have read too many books about Oxford or perhaps Harvard. They have insisted on recreating a fiction, but it has been to no avail. Academics tried for decades to copy those books, but seem now to have given up the enterprise entirely. I expect them soon to give up books. A portion of the student body already has.

CYRIL: But surely we both can spot an academic in a variegated crowd. When I look in the mirror or look at you . . .

VIVIAN: My dear fellow, do not impose upon our long friendship!

CYRIL: I beg your pardon. What I mean is that we are recognizable to each other, so there must be an academic style. We are infamous, at least among ourselves, for turning trivial and good-natured conversations into long-winded lectures. We answer questions with tedious explanations or longer questions. We see more sides to an issue than it should have in polite company. On certain subjects we cannot be turned off. We employ vocabularies not readily understood. We call our dogs and cats "Footnote" and "Ibid" or name them after the Brontë sisters.

VIVIAN: I congratulate you on your summary, but that is all mere appearance. If it is a style it is the decay of style. It is a decadence that has followed upon a fiction that never was. It demonstrates how hopeless it is for nature to endeavor to copy an ideal. As I have written elsewhere, it simply cannot rise to the really important occasions.

CYRIL: Oh dear, you have a strange look in your eye. I have seen it once or twice before.

VIVIAN: Yes. I confess that I am enamored of my formulation and feel another lecture coming on. The academic has good intentions but he can never quite bring them off. Perhaps there was a style to which the academic aspired. If there was, it possessed some of the characteristics of the oracle, the bishop, the club member, the amateur golfer, Henry David Thoreau, and Sir Kenneth Clark. It was, of course, an impossible ideal, a self-contradictory set. I have known several academics who have managed the first three, but none who could pass from them to Thoreau, let alone Sir Kenneth. And beyond all this there was the vow of poverty—easy enough in itself, but to play the club member and amateur golfer on the salary was simply too much. All that possibly could be achieved was a sort of genteel seediness—at the very best an untidy Lord Clark, if that can be imagined—with egg on his tie. No, Cyril, there has never been a *real* academic *Style*. Indeed, if you observe the faculty at their various bag lunches or in the cafeteria, you grasp at once the meaning of dowdiness.

CYRIL: That seems to me too harsh.

VIVIAN: Of course. It was meant to be. The cap and gown should be revived, not as a sign of academic splendor, but as a cover for the embarrassment of shabby tastelessness, an embarrassment the academic does not feel, so habituated is he to his squalor. Not too much can be done to vulgarize a gown. Oh, I suppose the young might take to Coors and Honda decals on their backs and electrified twirling tassels. Perhaps it is not a good idea after all.

CYRIL: That is the first time I have seen you lose your self-possession.

VIVIAN: It is a sign of the times.

CYRIL: In any case, to see the gowns in daily use would take something away from, or unfortunately add something to, processions such as these.

VIVIAN: No, that has already occurred. Look at their feet as they pass by. The boots, tennis shoes, sandals, and thongs that you see below you, protruding beneath the gown's hem, have already debased its style. But, yes, I believe you are right. To wear the gown only at convocation and commencement gives the whole a much-desired air of unreality, that *illusion* of *Style* which the faculty would surely corrupt if it occurred every day.

CYRIL: But surely you do not claim that there are no recognizable styles within academia.

VIVIAN: No, as a matter of fact, I believe our ability to recognize each other sometimes, for it is really no more than that, in crowds, as many animals do, is not instinctual but results from the existence of a family of styles, like Wittgenstein's word families. It is a chain of relationships that binds us together, but not each to each. Therefore, there is not one universal characteristic among us. I actually know a few professors who do not lecture your ears off, and a few merchants who do. Indeed, we may soon see a whole generation of academics who cannot lecture at all and will sit with other people only in a circle. You may be interested to learn that I am writing a monograph on this subject. It is called *The Decay of Style*. Would you like to hear what I have done so far?

CYRIL: Yes, with the Vivaldi they are playing in the background. By all means proceed.

VIVIAN: The principle I intend to establish is that academic life displays a number of recognizable styles but little or no *Style*. I shall pass over a passage that our conversation has already summarized, state a fundamental concept, and then proceed to a deduction of the styles.

First, the fundamental concept: the academic finds a style only when the style has passed. How else to explain the history professors' discovery of white turtlenecks for formal occasions after nearly everyone else had given them up? Perhaps they attended some gigantic Friends of the Library rummage sale. I have noticed subsequently a few in the College of Business Administration. Even poets rarely wore them during the revival of a few years ago. I believe that the historians will be the last to shave off their beards as well. Yet these are peripheral matters. One can't really *expect* historians to be up-to-date, can one? It would amount nearly to a contradiction in terms. It would be as if a professor of medicine made a nonanatomical joke, as if a German professor did not announce his joke, as if a French professor did not pretend he had made no joke, or as if a mathematics professor were not puzzled. It would be against art, to say nothing of nature, which some who have given the matter less thought than I believe academic life is against in any case.

There was a time when the styles were few, recognizable, and regional. There were principally four, epitomized by the Ivy Leaguer, the Southern academic gentleman, the agricultural Midwesterner, and the hunter-fisherman. As you see at once, each of these was in truth the copy of an image that had been created by novelists and thence corrupted. The Ivy Leaguer's Oxford-gray flannels and tweeds made him a cross between a spruced-up, considerably cleaner, and somewhat gaudy Oxford scholar and a Madison Avenue professional. The style often contained an Anglophile component, likely to be terminal after a prolonged stay in Britain. Such a creature whom fate had sent to some other area tended to consider himself much as a British colonial civil servant did in the previous century. He developed careful routines to preserve his dignity, his sanity, and the proper conduct of life. He ordered directly from Brooks Brothers and L. L. Bean, and he departed for Maine or New Hampshire as soon after classes ended in June as was possible. His research carried him inevitably to the Widener Library at Harvard.

The Southern academic gentleman, though occasionally observed as far north as Princeton or as far west as Texas, tended to resist lengthy migration; he settled in for a long stay on one campus, got deeply into real estate, kept a good garden, and offered excellent whiskey to his guests. His accent lent a certain sweetness to his orations, though they were not without bite. His external appearance belied a formidable academic politican and infighter. If he seemed rather isolated and provincial, he knew his home turf like a book. Let no Ivy Leaguer attempt to upstage him there, for upon that poor soul he would whet his beak clack clack.

The Midwesterner was par excellence long-suffering about outsized institutions, buildings that looked like Minnesota linemen, and the attendant bureaucracy, before others knew the meaning of the term. He was given to business suits of most unelectric blue, went to the football games along with everyone else in town, and liked a good long evening party, beginning at nine, with drinks preceding and following a midnight dinner. He did not mind on these occasions drink-ing and showing it, and he danced with assistant professors' wives, sometimes creatively and sometimes simply with abandon. He knew very well that there was a big university out beyond his own department, but except for the football team, he avoided it as much as possible.

The hunter-fisherman, found west of the midlands, was acquainted with the brief local history, in the form of folklore. He had built his own ski or hunting cabin and had added on to his house without obtaining a building permit. He had seldom been to a national convention. He wasn't terribly comfortable in a coat and tie, but he wore them when social obligation required. He wondered why the Midwesterner and Ivy Leaguer were so anxious about whatever it was that was getting to them. He thought, "The hell with all that," looked out over his spread, and considered trading his horse or adding to the orchard. He wore a Western hat only to journey east.

But this comparatively simple fourfold world no longer exists, if it ever did.

CYRIL: Why do you say that, my dear fellow?

VIVIAN: Because the picture I have drawn is, of course, one that nature has only approximated. Surely you recall my essay on the decay of lying.

CYRIL: Indeed, but there you said that nature copies art.

VIVIAN: And never achieves it. Now I make the same claim for history. Academic life has never quite risen to the symmetry of my historical account of it. No doubt pure examples of my forms occurred, and even linger on today in academic backwaters not served by United Airlines, but the whole schema could not survive the expansionist years and the 747. In its place we find a range of styles that can appear anywhere, like the housing tract, but again without *Style*. One can't tell an Ivy Leaguer from a hunter-fisherman any more. We are left only with the ubiquitous, the dull and repetitious, and, one suspects, the quite ungenuine copy. It is a further decay of *Style*.

CYRIL: But what are these copies?

VIVIAN: Their images are the entrepreneur, the faculty politician, the radical, the union leader, the dilettante, the artist. These do not exhaust the list but are enough with which to cope before the procession ceases.

CYRIL: But surely these have existed before.

VIVIAN: Indeed—the politician, the radical, and a different sort of dilettante—and always with the dominant regional variability. Now there is only dreary sameness. It is like traveling from airport to airport. But let me continue.

The most ubiquitous is the entrepreneur. He is an academic idealist . . .

CYRIL: Oh, come now, that is hardly . . .

VIVIAN: Yes, a thorough idealist, and full of principle. His ideal is the refinement of teaching into pure research; therefore, he avoids teaching whenever he can. He is also a staunch believer in freedom and therefore insists on living according to his own schedule. He keeps in close contact with his institution by long-distance phone. The secretary forwards his mail promptly, and he always visits when he is in town. He believes devoutly in carrying forth the word; therefore, he lectures wherever he can for a modest fee, and he does not miss a convention or colloquium, where he has been known often to comment with vehemence on the sanctity of scholarship and liberal education, which his own universality of genius proclaims that he has had, though he himself admits modestly and with lowered eyelashes that he is still seeking it. He carries proof sheets of his latest work on his travels and excuses himself from certain gatherings with the announced purpose of tending to them. He knows intimately the plane schedule to and from Washington, D.C., where he has lobbied successfully for research funds. He knows where everyone is at any given moment and with whom each is negotiating for a position. He declares that he has been called upon for advice and has given it. At Nobel Prize or Pulitzer Prize time he suffers indigestion and dizziness. He may, in the present climate, have seen his best days.

The faculty politician treats his campus as if it were a small town, which, of course, it is, except for its city-sized incidence of petty and grand theft. He visits the courthouse daily, plays a round of cards at the firehouse, and talks with the minor dignitaries, who know that in committee work he can be trusted to view both change and stalemate stoically and sometimes with pleasure. He is capable of facing without desperation innumerable luncheon meetings and the grapefruit wedges and maraschino cherry that inaugurate them. He is able to wait out the windy oratorical flights of presidents, vice-presidents, and deans, and to make his point by way of summary and conclusion when everyone else is exhausted. He lunches at the faculty club in what some think is heroic disregard of gastric disturbance and others view as evidence of an interior as steel-like as what is evident outside. He has won a few and lost a few, and he has worthy opponents to whom he speaks cordially, with whom he lunches occasionally, and whose obstinacy keeps him amused. He is loyal to the institution, which he wears like a suit of clothes, somewhat unpressed with tones of blue and gray.

The radical communicates with his friends and sneers at all others, accusing them of a failure to communicate. His colleagues are for the most part out of it, and their thought captured in outmoded categories. His students are either with him or against him, and the institution is clearly against him, though it is paying him a salary commensurate with that of those whose souls, if there were souls, are captive to it. He has supported the Catonsville Nine, the Chicago Seven, the Seattle Six, and such lesser numbers as can be assigned; but he has declared their politics naïve. He eschews the vegetarians, the Jesus movement, the Sierra Club, whatever else happens to be around at the moment, and the Socialist party, as irrelevant to a true ecological politics that redistributes wealth, returns all power to the people, and among other things abolishes "publish or perish." He reaffirms his solidarity with the people by wearing blue shirts. At meetings of the faculty he speaks of the plight of the students as niggers and occasionally of the faculty as niggers, and urges control over their own lives, student grading of professors, the abolition of grades for students, student participation on all committees, and student votes on all matters of policy. He urges, on the other hand, attention to the real world; and he declares the irrelevance of all of these local matters. He defends the concept of tenure, and believes in the seriousness of things.

The union leader may possess some of these characteristics, but his style is on the whole his own. He is everywhere at once and calls everyone of importance at least once a week. He gives the president as much hell as he can—complete with questioning of his motivations—in the press and in public meetings, which he never misses. He is aware of his audience of colleagues, which he wishes to impress with his fearlessness in the face of administrative force. He meets with the president in private and enjoys the role of consulting chieftain in the corridors of power. In these moments he suspects, against his own moral being, and perhaps worries, that he may have more in common with the president than with his constituency. He has tried to give the real side of things to his classes, though with indirection. He believes the radical is impractical and ineffective. He is likely to have committed a social science.

The contemporary dilettante runs as fast as he can to stay in the same place relative to student fashion. But that place is always a little behind the pace. His talk is of the sort that was hip when "hip" was hip. Though his knees crack, he has learned to sit on the floor with legs crossed and to believe that everything will be all right. He has turned on and tuned out and then tuned in to rock and R. D. Laing. He has been into painting and pots, and before he left his wife to live with a young psych major who converted him to backpacking, he was deeply into organic gardening. He has more Pre-Raphaelite posters per square foot of office wall space than any two teaching assistants. He has studied to be a guru and is so regarded by some. He has written eight poems. He has been promised by a friend a chance to review a friend's book in the *New York Review*, but in the end he has been found to be suspected of male chauvinism and the exploitation of young women, even though he is getting ready to write a sympathetic article, sequel to his "Self-Realization Beyond the Archetypal Mother" of a few years ago. In meetings he rises, jewelry jangling, to speak softly in behalf of students against the trauma of grades and bureaucracy and for experimental learning. He is puzzled when administrators adopt the same jargon. No matter—for he has lost faith in language, which suppresses real communication. Instinctively he feels that it is time to move on, but with his publishing record the only likely direction is down or out—far out.

The artist (I am told that the poets have been given passing mention elsewhere) is not quite certain that he is really here, believing that some preposterous mistake has been made in the general disorder of things. He spent the one faculty senate meeting that he attended (cajoled by his dean for an important vote) in perplexity. He is known to have spoken on that occasion, but no one was quite able to grasp what he was getting at, and he recognized the futility of it all as he stood there. The experience affirmed his fundamental belief that a few words will do. But he has definite opinions, particularly about those who are his contemporaries. They are divided at any given moment into friends and enemies. The latter outnumber the former and would need psychiatric help, if psychiatry were any help. He believes the administration exists, because his dean has told him he had better believe it, and he has no more feeling against the administration than against crocodiles or sharks. He is a little astonished that it arranges annually for his support. He feels there is something oddly perverse about this and concludes that his academic activities should keep a low profile.

CYRIL: But, my dear Vivian, I do not recognize myself or you in any of the portraits you have, I must say, rather unkindly drawn.

VIVIAN: Do you really think they are unkind? I am delighted to hear you say that. It means that people will be offended at being left out and will recognize all the colleagues they respect. But you are correct. Neither you nor I is present. We are a disappearing species and may in fact never have existed. In any case, we can indulge in the fiction that we began to disappear when everyone abandoned the idea of *Style*. You and I, Cyril, relish life for thought's sake and art for life's sake. We wish to look not like a student but someone who once was one. We prefer Cézanne to a computer, Mozart to a time-and-motion study, and "Jabberwocky" to a session in the counseling center. We refuse to obtain permission of the vice-president for administration before we place a rug on our office floor. And we shall not attend retreats even if they are renamed "advances," as they probably have been and surely will be. We insist on our students presenting papers in a known language (and on time) and being able to perform simple arithmetical tasks. We much prefer that they do not smell.

CYRIL [*alarmed*]: Vivian, you are becoming excited. Come, the procession is ended, the Vivaldi is over, and the president is beginning to speak. Come inside where it is not so noisy and you will not be further distressed.

VIVIAN [*disappearing with Cyril into the library*]: Wystan Hugh Auden, where are you now that we need you more than ever?

ᗰᗰ Chapter 7 ᗰᗰ

BUREAUCRITICISM: WHAT'S WRONG AND WHY IT ISN'T LIKELY TO BE FIXED

IT WAS AUDEN WHO, in the poem from which the epigraph of this book was taken, wrote:

> *Thou shalt not worship projects nor*
> *Shalt thou or thine bow down before*
> *Administration.*

Thus are the battle lines traditionally drawn. Promising or not-so-promising young professors are occasionally said to have "disappeared into administration," never to have been heard from again—at least no sensible word. A deep estrangement seems to occur at once between the newly appointed administrator and his former colleagues. Even administrators who have made serious efforts to maintain a minimal teaching schedule and some connection with scholarly activity find themselves in an alien realm. The process begins at once. Colleagues treat the administrator differently. Old friends speak to him with elaborate circumspection, on occasion with irritating sycophancy, and sometimes with outright contempt or at least distrust. Often it comes to be declared that their old colleague has changed, is not really an academic at all, or is a failed academic. This contempt cannot be explained entirely by the Oedipal element described in Chapter 1, though that is most certainly in the nature of things. It has been built in other ways into the university in the course of time. Just imaginably, with an immense effort, very unlikely to be undertaken, something could be done about it.

The reasons for estrangement are variable, and any analysis of them requires practice of the art of bureaucriticism. First, there are the problems connected with size and with the psychology of growth. We all know that Western economy has for a long time been based upon the inestimable values of growth and development—to the extent that the process of growth has practically eliminated the profitable small business, which at some time it becomes more profitable to sell to a larger business than to retain. Today we see all about us the ravages of that set of values, and we struggle like a fly in the marmalade to escape their darker implications. The concept of the fundamental goodness of growth captured the realm of education as it captured almost everything else. Perhaps educators thought they had to go along. Certain economic forces that I am incompetent to analyze must have made the movement toward the consolidated or unified school district, the monster high school, and the multiversity appear to most an inevitability. In any case, the 500-student or 1,000-student high school was declared not economically viable (I believe that's the buzzword), and the large universities were made larger. One wonders what the forces really were that compelled this disastrous development.

Well, clearly there were people motivated by the honest desire to open education to all at whatever level. One can hardly quarrel with the motive. But one need only look at the typical high school or large university campus today to question the strategy of endless enlargement that governed the period of huge population growth. Why did it happen as it did? There are many reasons. I merely mention a few that strike me as rarely acknowledged. The first reason has to be the refusal to examine the darker implications of the concept of growth. It was convenient not to do so. Belief in the goodness of growth made the seeking of larger budgets excusable. Growth offered excitement to entrepreneurial administrators, gave them status and at least the illusion of greater power. It brings these where smallness and the drive to achieve quality often do not. I have wondered what the role of interscholastic athletics was in the drive to consolidate the smaller high schools. Certainly the version of big-time athletics that has developed must have been attractive to ambitious high-school coaches and high-school administrators (many of whom seem to have been coaches, that being apparently a common avenue to administration). But it is obvious that the larger the school, the smaller the percentage of students making the football team, and as a result, the greater the estrangement of the mass of students from it. Also, the larger the school, the more bureaucratic becomes any effort to maintain an effective intramural sports program. All of the folderol that accompanies big-time high-school sports must, in the long run, eat up savings, while fewer students participate.

The principal reason that seems to be given to consolidate into the monster high school has been the more ready availability of physical resources, which promotes the maximum use thereof. There is allegedly a more efficient use of library space, sports facilities, and all services which can be centralized. Duplication is avoided. Clearly, duplicated libraries are expensive, but they are also useful to ensure that the students learn to read something beyond Dick and Jane. In any case, I have rarely seen a library of any real account in a monster high school. Some private schools, with small, intelligently developed collections, give an excellent education. With all the effort to bring technological services within reach, there is little evidence that secondary education has been improved and some to suggest that something important has been lost.

I have mentioned the high schools here because trends toward bigness seem to have occurred there first. But the universities and colleges may have been partly responsible for the thinking that let it all happen. The colleges of education developed formal training in educational administration and helped to create and endorse the ways of the professional administrator. Educational administration seems to be a discipline that produces a management class separated philosophically and socially from teachers and scholars. Methodology and technology become its concern, and these are divorced from what we loosely call content or subject matter. Educational issues seem constantly to be reduced to arguments about techniques, or production, or products, rather than questions of *what* needs to be taught. The upshot is numerous pious clichés, such as, "We teach students, not ——— [fill in any subject]." The whole act of teaching begins to be treated in an intellectual vacuum. It is not surprising that this attitude leads to a view of teachers themselves as technological objects programmed to "facilitate" a methodology. Give precedence to these ideas, together with the concept of growth as progress, and you go a long way toward what we have today.

In any case, it is a wonder that anyone with intelligence devotes a career to fighting the lesson plan, the host of bureaucratic regulations forced on teachers, the mediocrity of scholastic administration, and the intellectual void that is the typical course in education, to say nothing of the problems of discipline that plague our huge schools.

We should know by now that technology, though in itself neither good nor bad but supremely inanimate, is usually costly beyond initial imagination, as well as often distracting. I have heard it claimed that technology frees teachers to concentrate on other things. This is a shibboleth that deserves to have been invented by IBM. If it really did free teachers, for the most part it would be in the manner that the unfortunate Luddites were freed from their livelihoods. In an age of technology classes are becoming larger, not smaller. Machines, as any junior-high-school student knows, are an educational bore, except within a narrow range where they are real research tools. As far as I can tell, at this point teachers use them mainly to make possible brief rest periods for themselves in a tiring day.

The reasons why a university should tolerate more than an enrollment of about 12,000 are few, and they are not very good. First, one might argue that a single administration can manage the larger enrollment, thus saving administrative costs. I doubt that this is the case. Large institutions seem to develop huge and expensive bureaucracies very rapidly. The result is the creation of a management class from which the faculty and students are inevitably estranged. And this class discovers ways to entrench and expand itself. Professional stress is greatly accentuated at the top, and among administrators the focus is too frequently all wrong—back upon their own self-perpetuating activities.

Second, one might argue that expensive equipment in the sciences cannot be duplicated everywhere and that in a larger institution a smaller nucleus of such equipment is sufficient, since it is more readily available to all those requiring it. But before accepting the monster university campus as an answer, it would be worthwhile studying just how many students actually use such equipment. So that I am not accused of special prejudice against scientists, let me suggest that the library presents the same problem. My experience tells me that great libraries have really been developed principally for faculty and graduate students. A small, well-selected library is adequate for most undergraduates, particularly if faculty members take an interest in its providing the *necessary* books for undergraduate courses. It is quite possible for a modest collection to serve a faculty well, though not without frequent frustration. The pressure for a more extensive collection is always present, but I suspect that an arrangement of three institutions of 12,000 students each, with only one possessing a large research collection, is more livable and governable and finally capable of better education than one institution of 36,000. What would be necessary is a different attitude among faculty toward their role. More of that later.

Third, there is the argument that advocates maximum use of the plant. It originates, I suppose, in the analogy between a campus and a factory. This argument takes two forms: run the plant full tilt as many hours of the day and days of the year as possible; and fill up all available space with buildings. While large corporations have been developing new and more spacious plants on more attractive sites, universities have come to look more like factories and have destroyed the open spaces and vistas of their campuses with parking facilities and buildings of cheap construction, which are promptly defaced by hordes of students who hate them.

These observations lead me to the fundamental Principle of bureaucriticism, which is that *public education practices economy at any cost*. The cost is not just beauty but alienation of the spirit—an unmeasurable diminution in the feeling people have for their cultural institutions. I hold out little hope for an overturning of this Principle. We would not be likely to deflate our huge campuses even if all that they contained were the hot air that emerges from the colleges of education, the office of student affairs, and in some measure everywhere else. The costs of physical demoliton would be too great, and administrators would fight for their careers, which include the careers of their underlings. I see light at the end of the tunnel, and it is black. Once a managerial class has developed in an institution, there are bound to be efforts at growth or at least self-perpetuation, and finally an activity like that of William Blake's woeful character Urizen:

> *Dark revolving in silent activity,*
> *Unseen in tormenting passions,*
> *An activity unknown and horrible,*
> *A self-contemplating shadow,*
> *In enormous labours occupied.*

Another unfortunate result of the monster university has been the breakup of the monster within the monster—the college of arts and sciences. Time was when this college was the heart of the institution and claimed responsibility for liberal education. But with evolution and stupendous growth, its head ceased to understand its tail, and a doughty administrative Wiglaf appeared to hack it into various pieces. One typical job rendered it into three pieces, known as Natural Science, Social Science, and Arts and Letters. Others did a more thorough hacking and produced five parts. Like any good medieval *wyrm*, each part took on a life of its own—grew its own head and crawled laboriously on its way. The cumbersomeness of the original beast enabled Wiglaf to make amazingly short work of it, and there were many pious claims that the poor creature simply had to be put out of its misery. Its head was unable even to find out what its tail had just done, let alone what it was about to do. But the result has been further bureaucratic multiplication, further estrangement of the various disciplines, and with a few exceptions a disciplinary turning inward and self-isolation. Most critical of all has been the virtual destruction of any concept of liberal education or even a reasonably unified outlook of any sort. In situations where some departments are as large as the whole college was twenty-five years ago, there has seemed to be no alternative to this dismemberment. But if the *concept* of the college of arts and sciences is important, the political *fact* of it may be even more so. Under that regime the dean of the college of arts and sciences represented the recognized central core of the institution. His was the largest domain, with the main responsibility for undergraduate education. Other deans had other roles. When the college was hacked to pieces, suddenly there were three or even five deans, all with diminished authority and *no one* with the sense of responsibility for undergraduate education as a whole. The deans of professional schools found their weight in the councils of power to be proportionally greater. It was everyone for himself. Responsibility was easily palmed off on the next higher level of administration—the vice-president for academic affairs, who in all likelihood paid little attention to matters of educational policy, was called a tyrant when he did, or didn't have any notion of the intellectual concept of the college of arts and sciences anyway. The result has been an intellectual disorder unparalleled in the history of higher education, where petty chieftains can make virtually any claim to attention and where apparently any dean's idea of what is good for the student is as good as any other's, no matter what his intellectual role. This situation does not really enhance the power of the central administration, which keeps increasing its own size in order to be able to send out runners to try to discover what the hell is going on. The longer this state of affairs persists, the more people with nonacademic professional backgrounds will be accumulated and the greater the estrangement between faculty and administration.

Nowhere does this estrangement express itself more strongly than in the gulf that has opened between faculty and the large administration as the result of the development of the "student-affairs" bureaucracy. One does not know, in the dim dark history of these events, whether estrangement preceded the development of such administrative structures or vice versa. But one can conclude that *where there is a vacuum in the academic structure it will be opportunistically filled.* The process by which student-affairs bureaucracies have expanded independent of faculty concern and control is a by-product of rampant growth, "big" administration, and the estrangement of faculty from a sense of connection with or responsibility for the institution as a whole.

It was not long ago that an institution of reasonable size had merely a health center and a dean of students charged with disciplinary matters and with the management of a modest number of activities. How this arrangement eventuated in a vice-president for student affairs supervising a huge budget and a whole corps of assistant deans and lesser minions, with a corresponding proliferation of office space, bears some marveling. It is testimony to the American way. Offer a service, advertise it well, and soon some people will begin to think that it is not only appropriate and desirable but even necessary. This is what seems to have happened in the vast area of "counseling" which student-affairs offices have developed over recent years. The arguments that have been made for it boil down to three: the faculty is unconcerned and unavailable; the faculty is not expert in such matters; the modern university, like modern life, is so unresponsive and confusing that students need help. There is truth in each of these assertions, yet they may not be convincing enough, nevertheless, to justify the development as it has occurred. Faculty members are notoriously unavailable to students who do not arrange properly to meet with them. The very growth of a counseling program of which the faculty member is aware tends to alienate him from a sense of responsibility in such matters, even though he distrusts the counselors. The distrust is made worse when student-affairs officers, who seem to be legion and constantly publicized, are telling the students that indeed the faculty *is* unavailable and that it is lucky for them that someone else *cares*, and thinks the way they do (as opposed to those cold, unapproachable, intellectual ivory towerists). Thus the void is filled, because counselors will counsel on everything, including academic choices, marriage, careers, and improvement in interpersonal relations. They will be deep into things with fancy titles like "co-curricular learning," which sounds like an academic program competing with *the* academic program, and sometimes is, because as much as both sides speak of co-operation, both think in different ways. Each side believes it is busier than the other because each has a different vision of work. Student-affairs staff meetings seem to be rap sessions which are to be regarded as "co-curricular learning experiences" in themselves. A former student who had reason to attend one of these to present plans for a summer program for entering disadvantaged students has described his attendance to me. He was pressed for time and had to be at a class soon. Knowing the reputation of these meetings for endlessness, he asked that his matter be taken up at once. Suddenly everyone present threw a red poker chip on the table. This was a sign that he had been too aggressive. It was explained to him that there were white chips for whatever the opposite extreme was, and chips of another color for middle-ground behavior. After a while he left. Everyone seemed to be enjoying the session, and they were getting paid.

The great problem with counseling and the student-affairs efforts to enter the academic realm under the flag of education as therapy or therapy as education is the same as the problem harbored in the terms "education" and "educator." Such terms denote action but no substance. They stand for techniques and methodologies. Accordingly, they indicate flight from liberal education even as they pretend to assert its professed values. They represent what has been called the triumph of the therapeutic. The losers have been intellectual values. Here is a passage from a recent university catalogue, written to describe a student-affairs operation:

> Discussions with counselors help the student to identify issues and problems, examine values, discover strengths, talents and

interests, decide on actions and new directions, and improve
self-understanding.

After making allowances for the characteristic inanity of catalogue prose, and for the total absence of reference to a body
of knowledge to be learned, one might agree that these un-
deniably *Good Things* are part of what a formal academic education is supposed to accomplish. Yet one looks in vain elsewhere in the catalogue for similar high-sounding rhetoric.
Why?

Well, first, like happiness, such things cannot be directly
pursued; they are a by-product of learning the substance of
something. The academic withdraws from high-sounding assertions out of an entirely sensible embarrassment at their
naïveté, crassness, and overuse. One weary administrator
once told me that a catalogue ought to avoid *all* such statements of aims and promises of ultimate well-being: no one
ought to believe them. But, purged in one place, the tendency
to enunciate them seems to have turned up in another, as
ubiquitous as cow's bane or the necessity of obtaining a teacher's credential. Exploitation of the clichés of vaguely progres-
sive, fashionably radical pandering to the so-called youth
culture also falls to the peripheral campus service organizations, where what I called in Chapter 1 the therapies of the
moment are highly valued.

Thus, through the unfortunate division of labor, which
sends the faculty in one direction and the administration in
another, the way is opened for a subgroup of the latter to step
into the gap, declare or even create a whole domain of education as its province, and promulgate its implicit values. This
is done with administrative sanction—since the professed
aims are pious enough—and through channels which avoid
faculty authority, and with funding from student fees. The
whole business is distracting to the serious pursuit of scholarship, often faddist, and frequently antithetical to the intellec-

tual values the faculty professes. The rift is deeper than most faculty members realize, and few, alas, seem to care about it. To attack such high-sounding aims is to be labeled reactionary, antistudent, and ivory towerish. Yet the programs feed on and exacerbate these very tendencies in the faculty, and are not likely to change until the faculty changes deliberately. While some faculty members have donned jeans and beads, others gloomily predict that in the end their own colleagues will settle the issue by joining the therapeutic mysticisms in sufficient number to destroy education in any familiar sense. They argue that enough has happened along these lines already since the days of Dewey to render the outcome inevitable. They claim that the style of vaguely politico-radical-psychologistico consciousness-raising—which appears to be more or less the new Dale Carnegieism, or Life Will End at Forty Unless Each of Us Gets It All Together—is going to triumph completely in the classroom, as a generation trained in the mysteries of the rap session takes over the professoriate. In answer one can only muster the feeble admonition to trust in common sense.

The student-affairs bureaucracy cannot therefore be entirely or even principally blamed for a sickness that infects also numerous faculty members. Nevertheless, there seems to have occurred a deliberate or mindless creation by the administration of a synthetic pop counterculture inside the institution, with all of the clichés of such past movements given embarrassing sanction in the spate of publications emerging from it. The range of the student-affairs programs seems controlled only by the size of the budget. There are no limits to the possible number of services, learning experiences, and activities that may be imagined, and no criteria for exclusion or inclusion. Opportunism is made to appear palatable by calling it flexibility. Students become interns in the administrative structure designed in the first place to serve them. New offices with fancy names emerge, but no one can discover their functions. An office is created to obtain external grants for whatever the other offices do. "Out-of-class learning environments" and "personal and leadership skills development" programs are funded. There are "student-faculty interaction programs," which are inevitably described as virtuously "informal" and "ongoing," though most faculty don't even know they are going on. They are declared to have "broad-based appeal," apparently in contrast to the formal, narrow appeal of the academic program.

What are the fundamental issues generated here? My own ill-tempered view is that the university ought at least to put the student in a position to understand all of these things to be, at best, unfortunate signs of the times, like an epidemic social illness. The university is fortunately in spite of itself not a total failure in this matter; a number of students I know either have managed to reach a state of enlightenment about the disease or are endowed with a common sense that the university has not been able to talk them into abandoning.

I have suggested that the student-affairs bureaucracy tends to generate a demand for the services it provides. Oscar Wilde declared that there were no fogs in London until the artists created them. He was saying that man is responsible for how things are seen and, in that sense, for what actually exists. The university creates a lot of what the student perceives, and a great deal of care and thought should be expended before anything goes on the canvas. A Principle that might well be established here, though it is hortatory rather than descriptive, is: *Let the faculty be charged with creating such fogs as there are to be.* Some will be dreadful miasmal mists, but at least they will be the faculty's own and subject to sensible erasure in time.

Would it be possible to dismantle the student-affairs bureaucracy entirely and to direct the health-center psychiatrists to send home students who cannot cope, with instructions to their relatives to find help for them before they return? I doubt it. I suspect other forces make this impossible. Would it be possible to let the business office run the residence halls and to reinstate such rules of civilized behavior as would make them livable for a serious student who has learned the simple principles of hygiene and respect for the privacy of others? Maybe.

Under the present conditions of faculty and administrative behavior, the result would be a vacuum that a movement with worse academic values and even chancier therapies might fill. Therefore, the faculty would have to care enough to fill the vacuum themselves. How?

Probably no way. The effort would have to be fearless and heroic, and in the end the victory might be Pyrrhic. It would require a change of faculty heart, virtually a conversion of the spirit. The faculty would have to decide en masse or in huge number that the running of the university was their responsibility. Many claim this responsibility rhetorically when disagreeing with the president or the board of regents, but few (at least under present conditions) will actually assume it beyond the confines of their own department. Loyalty to the institution would have to equal that to the academic discipline. This would mean also that faculty would have to absorb the functions of administration to the greatest possible degree. This kind of change, of course, cannot be effected by violent revolution but only by decision of the board of regents and the current administration, which is unlikely to vote away its own powers. It would be necessary to continue to have an appointed president or chancellor, but that person's authority would have to be severely limited, preferably to ceremonial duties and public relations, including fund raising. The vice-president would be the real presiding officer of the institution, and he would best be elected from and by the faculty of tenured rank for a nonrenewable term of office long enough for him to accomplish something and short enough for him to return to scholarship and teaching only slightly impaired and with recovery possible. The same principle would apply to deans, chairmen, and other officers, including the vice-presidents (if any) for everything else. This process would eliminate nonacademic people from these positions, including those retired military personnel who have found havens in the educational bureaucracy, bringing some of their military values with them. All election to such positions would be from the inside. No one would ever be appointed to a faculty for the sole purpose of administrative service. By the same token—and this is the overwhelming problem—it would become necessary for faculty recruiting and, indeed, graduate education, to become more sensitive to the more general human competences. Graduate students would have to be taught about the running of universities—not as a major field, but as part of their professional preparation to teach history, engineering, or anything else. I feel that if some potential scholars rebelled against this arrangement, the loss to scholarship would be slight when measured against the gain. Perhaps, for example, the chores of keeping things going would not any longer be heaped relentlessly on a few. In most present departments it is well known that some people are dependable in class, in print, and out of both, and that others, though willing, can't be trusted. Further, some just don't give a damn, and others have been trained to tunnel vision. In most departments it is universally known who the latter are, but they are tolerated, along with just about everything else, because the tradition is one of academic freedom, which spreads conveniently over into *noblesse oblige*. And anyway, the criteria of faculty performance are militaristically stated somewhere and leave out the requirements of common sense and reasonable loyalty.

In order, then, to make the university function without the estrangement between administration and faculty, there has to develop a flow back and forth, an elimination of special bureaucracies insulated from faculty, and an adjustment in the expectations of faculty performance. A faculty member will have to assume that sometimes he will have administrative duties to perform. If there is to be a dean or vice-president for student affairs, he too had best be a faculty member serving for, say, three to five years. Certain people will more naturally than others gravitate toward doing service of different sorts, and in any system some will not be called. They will have slipped through the net or have changed, as people do. They should be regarded as mistakes. But they should also be regarded as the exceptions rather than as the norm or as those who have beaten the game. The pay-off for doing that should be eliminated.

Of course, it may be said that my cure is too violent and provides for no continuity. But in some areas it is working now, particularly where an efficient support staff exists to bridge the changes in chairmen and deans.

Perhaps you are saying—*doubtless* you are saying—that this chapter has contradicted the pretensions to universality of my earlier Principles, described originally as ultimate truths, and is ill-tempered to boot. Indeed, so it appears. The ill temper has crept up on me as it did on Vivian in Chapter 6, and I have indulged it. As for the contradiction, it should be remembered that when Plato finished his attack on the poets and banished them from the republic (though with garlands on their heads), he invited someone to prove his attack wrongheaded, since he admitted that he was enamored of poetry but could not find in his system a place for it. So every system closes itself and pays a terrible price for its perfect symmetry. Let my own bureaucriticism defy the system I have set up. But let no one imagine that I expect the solution I have offered to be attempted. It would require too strenuous an effort, even ruthlessness, and a massive change of attitude. The past decade has shown that universities have a way of persisting and of resisting sudden change. In many respects this has been a saving inertia rather than a fault. But that power of self-protection also allows for the perpetuation of obvious flaws and the creeping in of subtle mediocrity. The proposals I have made are not likely to be tried. I'm not sure I can say how they could best be attempted, nor can I guarantee that this best effort would not be quixotic. Therefore, my Principles stand. Still, . . .

Chapter 8

CONFESSIO AMANTIS

IT IS TIME TO CONFESS. It is in the proper spirit of the times to do so, even for someone like myself, now merely a former administrator. It is part of a deterioration that has accelerated since Auden penned the poem I have quoted. Confession is now *expected* of an administrator, whom the faculty regards (at considerable distance) as either (1) a poor beleaguered former faculty member fallen into the vortex, for whom sympathy must be shown to his face and contempt to his rear, or (2) a self-aggrandizing, ambitious, usually dictatorial politician who never understood academic life in the first place.

I readily confess that as I ascended the administrative ladder, each time charmed with the prospect of at last getting *something* accomplished (since in my previous role I had encountered bureaucratic tangles that seemed always to be frustrating my most cherished plans), I accumulated only the appearance of greater power. At the same time, my intimacy with the institution and its people lessened. I became regarded even by close friends as a being apart, as a creature to be managed, or worse, someone whose vanity had to be stroked. I discovered that the diminishment of intimacy seems almost to have been planned (in the great irrationality of things) to enable administrators to live more easily with the unpleasant acts of power that they daily must perform, while at the same time it makes them less certain of the actual necessity of such acts. I confess that in this situation, which I do not wish overly to dramatize (since even a former academic administrator should not be self-serving), I was on occasion able to assist some enterprising professor or chairman in an apparently worthy scheme, but I rarely succeeded in making academic policy. I sought ways in a busy schedule to teach and to keep up with my scholarly field, but each year with less grip on a constantly changing subject and with an unpleasant sense of growing fraudulence. In short, I found that I could sometimes facilitate, but less often create; that I could sometimes wind or unwind red tape, but less often cut it; that I could sometimes urge, but rarely command; that I could sometimes sympathize, but rarely cure; and that I was probably losing touch.

These conclusions, however, suggest that some modest achievements are possible. For a faculty to do well what it should requires reasonable calm on the one hand and a sense of activity and progress on the other, a sense of sympathetic leadership on the one hand and a certain amount of persuasion on the other. It is possible for me to confess to some success here, but as I receded farther into administration my sympathetic leadership probably grew more fraudulent. Indeed, I may no longer have been able to distinguish the fraudulences from genuine acts. I do know, however, that my confidence in achieving a desirable academic goal was progressively shaken by contemporary trends. The reason for this is that I believed, and still believe, in something I archaically call liberal higher education. (Dare I employ such an archaism, the acceptable term today being "general postsecondary learning experiences"?) Such an ideal is now characterized as elitist, reactionary, racist, sexist, perhaps vivisectionist, certainly counterrevolutionary, and (to create my own barbarism) publish-or-perishist.

I confess to believing in and actually using "teaching aids," but the one I like by far the best is the book; I even believe in educational technology, the technological object I most value being the book. I confess to arguing for educational "innovations," the one I most support being the teaching of the arts of reading and writing to undergraduates, as well as history, literature, and philosophy. I have even argued that it is time for these innovations to be tried out seriously in our primary and secondary schools in place of whatever is going on in them now. I believe professors ought to insist loudly on this in order to lend help to those beleaguered primary- and secondary-school teachers who still fight the good fight against heavy odds. The teaching of reading and writing is the teaching not of "skills" but of the arts of life, and cannot be separated by methodology from the development of coherent views of things, cannot be abstracted into "composition," "communication," "self-expression," or "consciousness-raising." Nor can a university of the sort that I have been concerned with in this book—a major university devoted to scholarship and research—respond to those criticisms that arise periodically concerning its impracticality, its inability to *train* students for the available jobs and the professions of the moment. The university is, in this respect, properly a conservative institution. It conserves and extends the positive forces of intellect and creativity in the culture, and is therefore properly uninterested in skills as "skills" or in professional advancement as a source of individual gratification. Thus it must in the end not only teach but judge and certify competence. It must, in short (if you will pardon what have become, to some, obscenities), test and grade and require accomplishment of those it graduates.

I confess to believing that science also is not merely a method but a mode of thought and that higher education will be liberal, or liberating, only when students become thoughtful about the ethical and metaphysical implications of science and find their scientific studies more closely integrated with consideration of philosophical issues. But it will not be an administrator who will lead them, any more than it will be a little child responding to his feelings or an adolescent insisting on control over his own life. The best an administrator can do is to encourage and urge the real intellectual leaders on a faculty to swell their ranks at every opportunity, to talk with each other, to enlarge the scope of the disciplines, not to destroy those disciplines in the vague, sentimental murk that tends so often to pass for "interdisciplinary" and "innovative" curricula these days, and to take real responsibility for the whole of their institution. I believe in the value of interdisciplinary study, but it must be inter*disciplinary*.

I confess to being bored nearly to death by the shrill claims made against the so-called "publish-or-perish" syndrome. A faculty of committed research scholars and creative artists is my idea of the most desirable academic community. I have yet to hear of a better way to see that an academic institution is intellectually alive than to assure that such activities go on, are supported, and help to create ideals of intellectual and artistic accomplishment. One doesn't have to assume that *all* research is worthwhile to hold this view. I confess to believing that academic institutions cannot be all things to all people and that some people do not belong in them. I doubt that we can tell who those people are merely by testing them. I fear prolonged sojourn in administration may cause people to lose these views, if they have them, not because they are naïve but because it is easy to be swayed from intellectual commitments when one is fighting fires most of the day. Therefore I believe that an administrative career should be relatively short.

I have learned a few things that chasten me on return to faculty status. I now have to admit when I face the administration that some of the faculty are cowardly or self-centered or willing to make scapegoats of administrators and students (or all of the above), that some have advanced intellectually but have remained emotionally adolescent, that many, under the present conditions of both faculty and administrative work, would soon tear their hair out if placed under the stress of an administrative post and forced to do what I have done daily, that every faculty generates deadwood and proceeds to petrify it and protect it against the best interest of true scholarship, while blaming the administration for lack of standards, and that academic life, though creating a gentler beast on the whole, does not ensure humanization of that beast.

I was amazed to discover myself acting rather like a right-wing Republican when the government increasingly imposed its deadening procedures upon me and my overworked office staff. I do not like the sorts of reports and mindless, stultifying categories imposed by the government in the name of accountability. I have been acrimonious toward the spate of acronyms with which I had daily to cope—WICHE, NCHEMS, NIH, NEH, NSF, HEW, and those generated by my own institution. I am astonished to discover that I created a few of these myself. I am disheartened by the heavy-handed practices that I was asked to administer in the name of "Affirmative Action," and I wish it were possible to achieve the meritorious ends of such action without them, though I have learned too that there are pressures against such change that I had not expected, and I realize now that good faith is not enough. I think that students can spend their time better than in serving on faculty and administrative committees, the virtues of learning-by-doing to the contrary notwithstanding and despite all that business about control over their own lives. As an undergraduate I regarded student government as farcical and the refuge of asses, and my view, though somewhat softened on the latter point, has not changed with respect to the former. I confess that I do not believe an academic community can be a people's democracy. Still, I recognize that student presence on some committees of the university has been beneficial and should continue.

Finally, I confess that I believe in the value of *formal* education (even the large lecture), and I am not embarrassed when the chairs in my classroom are not arranged in a circle. I think that the contemporary shibboleths of informality and sentimental egalitarianism in matters academic put off the day of maturity, to say nothing of judgment. Perhaps it can be said that I have been to the mountain and seen only the backsides of John Dewey. Perhaps I am sounding like Yeats's weatherworn marble triton among the streams. Actually I believe myself yet to be, after all these years of illusory authority, at heart an academic intellectual about whom the institution made some sort of mistake when it brought me into administration.

Therefore I declare that I am not yet totally depraved. My confession I regard as that of a lover of this profession. In any case, let the faculty member or the administrator without sin cast the first stone!

A TRIPTYCH
OF APPENDIXES

A POLITICAL PRIMER
FOR THE CHAIR
OF ENGLISH:
FORM AND CONTENT

THIS PAPER DIVIDES somewhat artificially into a discussion of
form and content in matters involving department chairs vis-à-
vis creatures like deans, review committees, vice-presidents,
and the world beyond the department generally. I don't deal
specifically with presidents and/or chancellors, since in my experience such people rarely if ever come within the chair's ken;
when they do, they are uncertain to whom they are speaking.
All this is to say that my observations are based only on personal experience and may or may not have any application to
the affairs of institutions I know not of and to which I am
certainly not going to fly in order to find out about.

I begin by repeating a principle that I stated on page 44:
"Debate over requirements deteriorates more rapidly the higher
the level of administration at which the debate is carried on." I
wish to revise this to say that "discussion of any intellectual
matter deteriorates more rapidly the higher the administrative
level." The most basic level of debate, and the best in academe,

goes on in the individual professor's mind when that professor is either working as a scholar, preparing for a class, or actually engaged in teaching. By the time we rise up to the scale as far as the professor's meeting with a chair, deterioration has already set in. In many departments neither party knows whether to condescend or fawn. When the chair meets with a dean, it is unusual that any significant *question* of education or scholarship should even be mentioned. Both people have been engaged in fire-fighting most of the day. They have been harried by the failure of xerox machines, sudden pregnancies in the secretarial staff, excessive use of the long-distance telephone, the unaccountable disappearance of teaching assistants, sobbing students, confused parents, suspected plagiarists, sexually indiscreet colleagues, quarrels with the bookstore, faculty members infuriated by the parking office, and requests for statistical reports. These last, it must be admitted, can be made into excuses for imaginative acts (though of a somewhat trivial nature and base intent), since they should involve what Sir Philip Sidney called an improvement on nature and can only be interpreted as some weird test of the chair's prowess. One suspects that the psychology department is behind them and is devising a new way to test imaginative power.

It is up to the chair to raise the level of discourse with the dean, for the dean is not likely to do so. The academic principle in operation here is that the next highest level of authority should always be regarded, though fondly, as somewhat imbecilic. It must always be remembered that the dean was once intelligent and has suffered impairment of vision only as he or she has risen to higher levels of abstract power. Occasionally a mistake is made, as in the following poem:

The Rhinoceros Who Became Dean

Since it required a scholar, critic, fiscal wizard, and
   all around tough guy besides his being a,
   you know, well like a real human being who really

relates to students, y'know what I mean?
they gave up and made the rhinoceros dean.
The trouble began at once because
    he preferred the grass in the campus park
    to munching the paper that
    the ditto machine fed him,
    the elevator was too small,
    and the secretaries misunderstood
    his horn.
Besides, on the first day an impertinent
    coffee machine failed to dispense sugar
    and he butted it in a rage,
    a new trailer for fifty teaching assistants
    was placed directly over his favorite mudhole,
    and at least thirteen coeds
    on thirteen separate occasions
    offered him peanuts without fear.
    He was not a goddamned elephant!
And to prove it he ate at high noon
    all the salads in the Commons,
    fifty cellophane wrappers containing
    whatever was in them,
    and a platter of apples.
By early afternoon he had attracted
    an active following who urged him
    to advance next door on the
    card catalog.
Like the elevator, the library entrance was narrow,
    but he burst into the foyer and ate
    all the way to G before
    the vice-chancellor took his name
    and learned his intention was Z
    and after that the subject index.
Properly identified, back in his office,
    ready for his first interview with the *Register*,
    he was prepared to concede that maybe
    they should have picked
    an animal from the outside.
    A carnivore perhaps.

An unusual choice, made in desperation.

Let me enunciate six principles involving relations with the dean or others above:

1. *The dean, particularly a new dean, may be quite ignorant about the discipline that a chair represents.* I once heard a dean who was keen on quantification say that he saw no reason for a new institution to build a library. Everything would be information retrieval systems. He was a dean of social science, thank God. Another dean once expressed astonishment to me that humanists did research, thinking that all they did was "read books." These are perhaps discouraging examples that suggest imbecility and little prospect that one's dean can be trained to more than simple tasks. No doubt they exaggerate the problem. In any case, the only hope is for better things. There is no reason in the world except deep pessimism, fear, and trembling why a chair should not, with tact, set out to educate the dean to the nature of his or her discipline. It is, of course, a dangerous undertaking. In this case, too much knowledge is a dangerous thing. An Irish wag once said, "We Irish have so much respect for learning that we rarely dare to approach it." That, of course, is the situation one strives for in a dean—respect at a reasonable distance. A dean should be taught to understand not only a department's scholarly concerns, and the major issues in the field, but also the pedagogical facts of life. A dean with some understanding in these matters will be easier to approach in a crisis (though, of course, this is not the time to approach a dean). Deans will surely find a way to make use of the knowledge you offer them. They didn't rise to their positions with their ears plugged, only with their mouths shut. This is only to say that deans are as vain as anyone and will display their learning when they feel they are on solid ground. Further, we must trust to the belief that the whole academic enterprise cannot be harmed by a dean who knows what he or she is doing. In short, chairs should educate their deans.

2. *Deans are often actually attracted to intellectual issues when the rare opportunity for dealing with them occurs.* Deans are often

people made intentionally lonely by their roles. They would like to make sound decisions on intellectual and educational principles, but issues brought before them have suffered deterioration of the spine. Further, their own principles are often derived wholly from their own disciplines and may well need broadening or gentle questioning by application of the rhetorical devices of antithesis and cacaphony. A chair is responsible for doing that.

3. *In any group of chairs under a dean, certain ones, maybe only a few, stand out.* By undefinable characteristics of personality, perhaps. By adoption of a Yeatsian mask. To mimic Maud Gonne, surrounded by bird cages, is probably a mistake. Yet a chair must find ways to make his or her voice heard and to draw respect. This is why it is a great advantage for a department to present to its dean a chair who has scholarly authority and acknowledged intellectual power. A chair ought to find ways to keep up scholarly activity. (Incidentally, such a chair ought also to make colleagues respect the administration function more—a needed change. But of that I shall speak later.) This matter makes application of principle 4 easier, namely:

4. *The principle of the squeaky wheel.* No department can expect to prosper if it does not make some noise. The question is: What kind? With some regret I must say that the squeaky wheel principle seems to work. But only if it is relentlessly applied. The most successful dean I have known was characterized by his chancellor as a "cry baby," but he got more from that chancellor than anyone else. Perhaps after a time he was overdoing it. I don't know. (Yeats's friend, John O'Leary, said there were things one shouldn't do to save a nation, and one of these was to cry in public.) This dean was greatly revered, and much of his crying was in behalf of good sense. Threats, on the other hand, are always mistakes. Wheel-squeaking is to be done with restraint and requires an entertaining personal style.

5. *Horn-blowing.* It is axiomatic that no one will blow a department's horn if the chair doesn't. In the great fog which is

the universal condition in which funding is allocated, the horn is necessary if the upper administration is even to locate you. No strength or accomplishment, individual or tribal, must go untrumpeted. A dean who has some idea of what your department does is better equipped to hear the horn. Therefore return to principle 1.

6. *In the end, though, what a dean wants a lot of is peace, not pests.* Departmental internal order means a great deal to the dean, even if at times he or she may appear to act as though he or she were seeking to stir up strife. If a department can solve its own problems, that's the best thing, and this leads to some other principles—those of internal policies.

Some years ago a wise retiring chair told me that the key to departmental morale was to find ways for everyone to have some specific responsibility and thus involvement. He said it was not always easy to involve certain people, but it was better for them to be dithering responsibly than to brood in isolation or resentment. I have combined that advice in my memory with the story told to me of a commander of a ship during World War II who insisted that every one of his officers know how to dock the ship. He would take the ship out into the bay, leave the bridge, go to his cabin, and sit on his bunk with his head in his hands until the operation ended. Anyone who adopts this policy must be able to tolerate a certain amount of inefficiency and even be prepared for a disaster of minor proportions. There should be in every chair's mind a certain number of lesser but interesting tasks that give at least an aura of importance to those involved.

I'll enunciate two other principles of internal politics before passing from form to content. First, a chair should campaign for what he or she wants done, counting the votes, making sure the time is ripe. The worst experiences departments have are acrimonious formal debates that end in no action. Not that matters of import shouldn't get out in the open! But let them be ones worth the trouble. Second, the chair should be *available*, even at the expense of efficiency. Do not tolerate a protective secretary—the sort that so infuriates you when you call your physician.

I now turn to content. What are the matters before chairs that need particular attention these days? We all know that things have changed, and even faculties are finally *acting* as if things have changed. Things are back to something more like normal after the peak of excess in the late sixties. At a recent convention of publishers it was announced that only 0.64 percent of the money allocated for education in America is spent on textbooks, and that figure is declining. There will be 3.9 million fewer students in the next four years. The purchase of textbooks will decline by 6 million units per year. The total number of all books published is declining. Fewer than 5 percent of the adults in the United States buy books. I felt the pinch this year. I was teaching a course in Joyce Cary, and all of his books are out of print in this country; some are in England. Other matters: The *Los Angeles Times* reported the other day that one-third of the eighth grade in San Bernardino was being held back because of failure on reading tests. A similar phenomenon occurred in Chicago. Among freshmen admitted to the University of California, about 60 percent, I believe, cannot pass the entrance examination in English and must take a remedial course, for which there is now agitation to give credit. This is not a phenomenon to be explained entirely by racism and poverty. The worst percentage in the University system was, I believe, achieved in the freshman class at Irvine in Orange County, where the average cost of a home is now $107,000. [These statistics are dated 1977, the year in which this essay was written. Homes in Orange County cost a lot more now. The other statistics may still be accurate enough.]

The economics of book publishing alone may insure the triumph of the dean I knew who was against new libraries; but if it does, we shall have cooperated in our own demise. Years of public largesse and growth corrupted us. There were *so many* students and *so many* jobs that we assured ourselves and the public of many things. For one, our students were supposed to be the brightest ever. They didn't need those old basic, irrelevant courses and requirements, and we could concentrate on specialized advanced work, whatever appealed to us at the time. We could politicize our offerings and under the guise of interdisciplinary freedom or relevance turn our own work into soft social science. Supermarket education was triumphant, and among humanists so was amateurism. Many of us even decided to try to join the majority, i.e., youth, and adopt their dress, manners, and undeveloped taste—if one mentioned taste, which was, of course, a bourgeois concept. After all, the imposition of standards in a discipline was racist, capitalist, probably sexist, possibly vivisectionist, and in any case neither cool nor *au courant*.

It wasn't until the squeeze on budgets and jobs that English departments miraculously rediscovered the woeful preparation of entering students. Then the hue and cry was heard throughout the pages of the *Chronicle of Higher Education*. Then, too, the scientists began to complain in earnest (instead of merely to grumble) about how overhead money from grants was drained off to humanists. When the going gets rough the scientists will assert their power at the humanists' expense.

All this is to say that the chair must recognize that humanistic values are in an embattled position. An English chair's principal political task is to fight back imaginatively. No one is going to do it if he or she does not. English departments represent the largest and most diverse group of humanists on campus. They have the opportunity to touch the most students. For the most part, physical and natural scientists think very differently from humanists about education and the academic world. Social science in its dominant aspects threatens to destroy the humanities by swallowing them. Many of us seem unable to resist this embrace, which comes in various forms— structuralism, the human sciences, and the various ideologies accompanying these movements. In the past few years, review committees on my campus have been dominated by people most of whom haven't the faintest idea of humanistic scholarship, how it is produced, and what form it takes. Further, the capacity of such people to *think* they know all about what we do is considerable. I know a French department that is harassed by professors in the sciences trained in France, who really think they are experts in the department's affairs. They have a sentimental, amateurish view, but they make themselves heard. All this is to say that English departments must do it for themselves.

I offer eight points, among any number that might be elicited, for consideration—practical points of content. They all have to do with the establishment and maintenance of departmental power, which for the foreseeable future is the business chairs are in:

1. When I taught at Cornell, Texas, and Michigan State, there was in those institutions a required freshman English course of one year's duration. It was regarded as an important course, but it seems to have died from affluence in many places. The chair should fight for its reinstatement where it is not universally required. Then annually, at some appropriate time when the department is assembled in solemn conclave with its graduate students, the chair should give a public oration in its praise. The ceremony should end with a singing of the hymn:

> O Comp[osition], our help in ages past,
> Our hope in years to come,
> Our shelter from the stormy blast,
> And our eternal home.

2. Since the return or enlargement of freshman English requires more teachers, propose a plan in which an increase in
regular faculty is the best educational choice. We all know that
American universities are putting forth more Ph.D.'s than the
job market can absorb. It would be folly to increase the number of TA's and graduate students to teach freshman English or
anything else. Further, the quality of TA teaching is relatively
low and a major source of complaint. The only choice is to
demonstrate that ultimate economy has been practiced in the
department by strict reorganization at all other levels and that
more, but not enough, faculty are going to teach freshmen.
This is a development devoutly to be hoped for by students,
parents, legislators, regents, and high administrators, at least
in my state. An effort in this direction is the only way I can see
to generate even the possibility of new junior faculty positions
in a period in which jobs are so scarce. It may be that to argue
this point may only prevent attrition, but that is a good, if
modest, goal in some places. The task of the chair here is a
slow one. Years of denigrating freshman English by the people
who are responsible for it must be overcome. The program
could involve some loss of TA's, deliberate shrinking of the
number of graduate students, and a change in the faculty's
work day. The last is a tough task.

3. Since we live in language and argue among ourselves
whether people speak language or language speaks people, English chairs ought to be supporting as stiff a foreign language
requirement as possible. Certainly it is through acquaintance
with a second language that one comes in part to speak language rather than, in one sense, to be spoken by it. As far as I
know, the last gasp of this requirement occurred at Michigan
many years ago, where the event was simultaneous with re-
surgence of the football team.

4. Students simply do not know what to do with an English
major. The variety of work English majors get into and do well

at is immense, and departments should be able to document that and distribute the results widely. At the very least, a pamphlet should be developed, readily available and perhaps sent to all freshmen, on the subject of what professional roads are available to English majors and why. Examples of programs for English majors combined with pre-law and pre-medical programs should be included. If the department can't develop such a document, get an engineering professor to work out a neat four-year chart. The pamphlet can feed, in part, on the MLA publication entitled "English: The Pre-professional Major" of a few years back and still in print.

This is merely a specific example of ways to argue publicly for the value of English study. The argument must be made far less arcane than we have recently been making it. On this point, Mathew Arnold still has something to say to us. But we needn't stop with him.

5. In politics, one party follows another around with so-called truth squads. A chair needs to create a few of these within the department in order to deal with external affairs. One should be constituted to make formal complaint against all local abuse of language and thought—by public ridicule and invective, if possible. After all, it is our language that the campus newspaper and high administration are slaughtering nearly daily. Instead of making jokes around the coffee urn about this, why not take up the verbal sword as did John Crowe Ransom's heroic Captain Carpenter? Quixotic? Perhaps. But who else is going to do it? And what *do* we believe in?

6. The department should publicly advertise and support the creative arts of writing on campus. There should be readings, competitions (both oral and written), journals, broadsheets, and even poetic duels in the old Celtic mode. Let the campus poets speak out on the events of the day. Every English department ought to have a small press and a course on the art

of printing and making books. In our time, we have seen poetry become more and more a specialized activity, isolated
from the community where most if it is made—the university.
Since the university is now the patron of most of the poetry
published in this country, it should hear that poetry, even when
the poetry bites the hand that feeds it, as it surely will.

7. There are not enough humanists in academic administration. The English department should always have a candidate
for all committee and administrative posts. If the department
can get together by caucus on a candidate (internal or external),
that is desirable. The visibility and voice of department members is important in an institution, much more important than
most members realize or even want to realize. One myth that
needs to be leveled is the one about the impracticability of
humanists; many humanists are very good at administration.
(I have to observe parenthetically that one of the problems of
the academic institution today is lack of commitment to it as an
entity that has a life to be protected. Every faculty member
ought to expect to contribute at some time, as a matter of
course, to the running of the institution. If faculty members
abdicate this role, others will assume it. Further, any graduate
program ought to have in its program a short course in academic life and politics for its students.)

8. Many universities draw most of their students from, say,
fifty high schools. We complain about the training of our freshmen but do little about it. Instead of complaining, what can we
do to help? This is a difficult business, but we could begin by
developing personal liaisons with English faculties in the high
schools which send us the most students. What each department should have is a squad of faculty that spends some time
on this matter every year. We need colloquia and exchange of
ideas and experiences on a personal level with high school faculties. This cannot be left to the office of relations with schools.
We need imaginative efforts in disseminating what we are about.

Many of these things take up faculty time, but they are all worth the time for long-range benefits to the humanities, the department, and in the end the individual faculty members. Faculties, like other groups, are enlightened as individuals but short-sighted as groups. The horse of instruction is not an entirely docile creature when prodded. It must be led, dear chair, but gently, gently.

HOW DEPARTMENTS
COMMIT SUICIDE

IN *The Academic Tribes* I offer a series of principles and antinomies of academic politics, which by way of introduction I
shall briefly restate here. They are: (1) The Diffusion of Academic Authority: No one has the complete power to do any
given thing. (2) The Deterioration of Academic Power: Real
academic power deteriorates from the moment of an administrator's first act. (3) The Diminishment of Organizational Allegiance: The fundamental allegiance of the faculty member
will be to the smallest unit to which he or she belongs. (4) The
Luxury of Principle; or, The Third Law of Academic Motion:
To every administrative act there is an equal and opposite reaction. (5) The Protective Coloration of Eccentricity: Eccentricity is not only to be tolerated in academic life, it is often
a positive virtue. (6) The Necessity of Symbolism: Faculties demand the proper maintenance of the symbols of their
institutions.

The antinomies: (1) The faculty are the university; the faculty are employees of the university. (2) The administration is
master of the faculty; the administration is servant of the faculty. In seven years [this essay was written in 1983] no one has
disputed these principles, and my antinomies have on the
whole fared better than Kant's: They have the good fortune to

be ignored or to be taken for granted, so I have easily mustered the temerity to offer four more principles that are this time devoted to the behavior of academic departments. These principles, unlike my previous ones, have a polemical and ominous quality that seems correct for the times. They should hold as admonitory advice to chairs as long as English departments survive, taking their places alongside the wisdom of recent decades that memorializes Parkinson, Peter, and the engineer who observed that if anything can go wrong it will. I offer my principles in logical order:

Principle the First: *An overworked and underfunded department has a greater chance for health than any other.* I do not offer this as Pollyanna, nor is it meant as a mirror in which you can all see yourselves. Clearly there are too many institutions on the edge of starvation and shocking exploitation of faculty. Still, it is a simple fact that many departments are thriving when they recognize themselves as being in a lean and hungry condition. Look at it this way: To enjoy a more saturnine state is inevitably to approach deanly dismemberment, to face the need to make appalling decisions that cause interest groups in the department to compete frantically for anything likely to remain. The impulse of each group is to develop first-strike defensive capabilities and use them on all the other kivas of the tribe. Only in the underfunded, overworked state can a department chair approach a dean and demand justice with all the weight of morality on his or her side. It is quite unlikely that anything resembling a beautiful goddess with scales in hand will appear. Most deans these days, being strictly empiricists, cannot summon up mythical belief. But there is satisfaction in being able to argue with one's dean a morally sound position and to come away yet again convinced of one's moral superiority. Furthermore, the problem will have been kicked upstairs for the time being. Corollary: *Everything in administration is for the time being.*

It follows that a situation in which one is not underfunded and overworked ought not to be allowed to occur. It would be an incompetence to see the possibility of balance and not avoid it. This is as axiomatic as the rule that one should never end the academic year in the black, unless one wants oneself to become a dean by the route of sycophancy. Indeed, a slight deficit is most desirable. Anything else is bad management. This only proves once more that the rules of academic life are political, not those of business.

Ultimately more important than achieving a deficit is the capture and ownership of symbols. One must maintain the power to define the terms one employs. One must be able to declare with authority and absolutely, for example, what being underfunded and overworked means. One cannot allow one's terms to float about in such a way as to be capturable by the dean's business manager. Nor is it advisable for a definition to be borrowed from any other department or to be consistent with any known deanly working formula. There must be a certain mystery in one's definitions, particularly in questions of class size and teaching load. Let me offer an example of how the establishment of one of these symbols can go wrong, even when one's own definition of appropriate class size has been accepted. For some reason not entirely clear to me, historians seem to welcome large classes. Perhaps it is in their character to want to deliver truth in the mode of pomposity learned from the political figures they study. Perhaps they want the luxury of avoiding dealing with their students' writing so that they can continue to deplore it and the effectiveness of the English department. This tendency to tolerate large classes is, I think, dangerous. Historians may be underfunded and overworked, but their definition of appropriate class size tends not to reveal this and as a result there has to be a diminution of their communal sense of moral superiority, though some historians may regain it as individuals whenever they contemplate a sea of bright faces before them. This does a department no political good. On the other hand, some smaller departments find themselves by the measure of class size overfunded and apparently underworked. Since they have little hope of attracting more students in the short run, it is clear that their best hope to become underfunded, overworked, and thus in this way safe from the ax is to enlarge their scope, invent new courses, advertise them, and thereby attract new students. Involved here, of course, is a definition of what they do, a capturing of a new symbol. I shall say more about this in connection with Principle the Fourth, for there are dangers in such strategies. Clearly the important thing is for a department to be able to declare the appropriate ways in which it works. This means that some things become unthinkable or nearly unthinkable about that department. This is something that cannot be achieved overnight and must be worked on communally, which is one reason it doesn't often occur.

I might add that many science departments work communally to define teaching load and admirably mystify it in the most effective ways, though the same strategy—if it could ever be discovered and reduced to rigorous principles—might not be workable for humanists without radical and perhaps undesirable changes. A humanities faculty member's teaching load is roughly definable in terms of courses taught. Some science departments succeed in applying the strategy of absolute obfuscation on this point, to the extent that even a dean's spies infiltrated into the ranks cannot return with a clear picture. Perhaps a team of humanists should be appointed to explore the advantages and disadvantages of principles of obfuscation for their own uses. The problem here, of course, is that humanists don't tend to work very well at anything in teams.

In short, to be underfunded and overworked is to be alive, to be planning constantly to escape such a state even as one knows the dangers of any other and have constantly in the back of one's mind ways to become underfunded and overworked in the unlikely event of a stunning success. In addition to ensuring a sense of moral well-being, such activity exercises the mind, sharpens one's sense of irony, and busies the faculty, thus decreasing time for less charming forms of activity, whether mischievous or morosely introspective, as humanists are often likely to be.

Principle the Second: *The usual strategies of department self-protection are self-defeating and can lead to suicide.* (One of the ways is to become evenly funded and evenly worked, as I believe I have just shown, but there are many other ways.) This principle is designed to apply particularly to departments in the so-called humanities and particularly to large departments like English, but I have come to believe that it holds throughout the institution. The most common and most pernicious strategy is to resist every possibility of reaching out beyond the department's so-called traditional boundaries. It must first be remembered that on the grounds of history alone English departments are relatively young phenomena and need not regard what they should or should not do as chiseled in stone. Nor did the originary department chair see the backside of God. The so-called traditional definition of what is central to a department is always passé once it has become possible to utter it in one hundred words or less, which is to say make it comprehensible to a dean. When this steady state is achieved it has already been time to move on, if only to maintain obfuscatory advantage—one of the few advantages (as I have already implied) that one enjoys over a dean. Generally some such passé notion defines the departmental major and under the standard of self-protection drives decision making. To protect the major becomes unfortunately synonymous with survival, and this in turn tends to limit opportunity for growth (if one wants that) and intellectual development (which surely one ought to want). To fall back and really rally 'round in this way is to harden into dogma the results of the violent revolutions of a previous generation of scholars and surely to lay the groundwork unknowingly for a new revolution, as violent as the preceding one, now forgotten. To build one's program and faculty entirely around protection of the major is almost certain to limit future possibilities, which are so often generated by fortunate chance or unexpected opportunities. Such closing in is found also in time to be erosive of student interest and respect. The history of classics in many institutions confirms this view. When a new infusion of imagination in classics departments led to a reaching out toward other departments and new critical approaches, classics reversed the trend. Recently, my own institution, under severe budgetary pressure, has painfully reviewed certain departments with the possibility of eliminating them. One of these departments, Near Eastern languages and literatures, was on the list. In this day and age, why? Well, the reasons for termination given by the administration turned out to be based on not very good information; upon review the decision was wisely reversed. But what caused this department to become a target in the first place? The main reasons were, of course, complex, involving basic misunderstandings and power politics outside the department, and the department's special internal history, but the department was never able to define itself in a way that helped. This internal failure generated over time a garrison mentality that saw no offensive strategy as possible. As far as I can tell the department didn't know how to demonstrate that it was reaching out and was important to the rest of the institution. Now, of course, reaching out must be done with imagination and dignity. Surely the department had its opportunity in the light of the importance of the Near East in the public eye today. But under siege the department retracted rather than regrouped, and it had to be saved by a massing of friendly external forces. Each act of self-protection had made matters worse.

Well, you may say, English is simply not in that sort of fix. Probably not, at least over the short term, but in many places in recent years there have been ominous events that if unchecked would have transformed the situation radically. The short-term problem for English is not survival but how to maintain a relatively quite favorable position. That is one way of putting it. The other way is: How to play the productive intellectual roles that English can and ought to perform.

Generally, the death wish expresses itself in English departments by (a) denigration and/or trivialization, often subtle, of the department's so-called service role, (b) relegation of some departmental programs to the periphery, (c) failure to give leadership (as a large department should) in the development of general education, (d) refusal to embrace new aspects of intellectual life that might well become or in part become the province of English, and (e) refusal to lead in areas where interdepartmental cooperation makes more sense than provinciality or aggressive colonizing. Let me take up each of these points briefly. There is no reason in history or in stone tablets to assume that literary study, regarded as the study of the great works of poetry, drama, and prose fiction, should be regarded as the center of English studies. There is no reason to claim that literature as an art is the center. That claim was refreshingly made by the New Critics at a moment in the history of all this when it was rightly perceived that the notion of literature as an art was being taught nowhere or in very few places and that it ought to be. There followed a gradual victory of this view—a victory perhaps too successful for the health of English seen as a congeries of disciplines. As a result, a natural and completely understandable reaction set in. By no means a matter entirely of competing critical theories, it was the rebellion of the other disciplines housed in English against the hegemony of an aesthetically oriented criticism. In other words, it was political as well as intellectual. Significant developments in linguistics and anthropology clamored for a hearing along with certain ideological movements. There is probably always going to be this kind of jostling. Whatever values or groups seem to prevail at any moment, there is a tendency to forget or try to forget that English departments perform a general intellectual role. They should do so with a sense of professional responsibility that they will not abdicate in the face of fashion. It ought to be a task at least as important as any other. Furthermore, departments should never again fail to recognize that the teaching of writing and the contribution to the literacy of the university community are the department's loaves and fishes in times of want. This was nearly forgotten in the heady sixties, when students were suddenly declared to have reached heights of literacy unknown to colleges in years gone by, and certainly not known since. In the preceding essay I wrote that freshman English (or some variation) is "our help in ages past / our hope in years to come / our shelter from the stormy blast / and our eternal home." Let our suicide not occur from our forgetting these most relevant of lines from that old hymn. Let us also declare that this is a responsibility that we had better not delegate or abdicate to other units that advertise quick and easy solutions. It would be irresponsible and it would be self-destructive. It would, of course, result in being overfunded and underworked.

There are other things that English needs to provide to the academic community and that the community needs. In today's theoretical and social climate it is difficult to articulate literary artistic values effectively and, of course, some theories reject such values as socially pernicious or irrelevant, viewing all writing as grist to the mill. From some points of view this is no doubt correct but from a point of view that does hold to a notion of artistic value or to the desire for verbal literacy and dexterity, it appears to me that Shakespeare ought to come before Winnie the Pooh. Some courses may produce the right statistics in the dean's office, but only if statistics call all the shots and only if the department wants to risk its credibility in more important matters over the longer haul. Courses in trivia send the wrong intellectual messages. This does not mean that children's literature or popular fiction should not be taught in a context of study of the verbal culture, but it does imply that they are not the best pedagogical introductions to literary study or ways of fulfilling a humanities requirement.

It is a mystery to me why we so often withhold from even our own majors systematic discussion of philosophical questions about our various subjects: What do we mean when we speak of literature? of language? Is there literature? About such questions we should have something to say. If we do not, we lose our sense of a purpose that can be explained and defended. Of course, literature, if it exists, is not our only subject. Language is also our subject—language in its theoretical and practical dimensions—though we must acknowledge that we are not alone in claiming it. We must, therefore, recognize our necessary relation to other departments with linguistic interests. No behavior involving language can automatically be ruled out of our interest, nor can the history of these matters or the teaching of earlier forms of English.

Traditionally, English departments have relegated certain of their own programs to the periphery of concern. For about forty years now, literary interpretation, roughly in the New Critical vein, has been the tacit center, though recently this center (and in literary theory all centers) has been called in doubt. Since English departments are composed of a variety of scholars practicing loosely related disciplines, it seems to me pernicious to declare as a center any one of them. When we have done so, the declaration has held for a few years at the expense of other things, sometimes with appalling results. First but not necessarily foremost has been the effect of stultifying the methods of the so-called center so that it becomes a still center. Second, there has gone along with this the imposition on other kinds of scholars the standards of promotion of the prevailing mode. Recently in my own department, an assistant professor who specializes in teaching English as a second language and directs the program was denied tenure, not by the department, which (I am happy to say) overwhelmingly supported him, but by a higher review body that proved its own incompetence and prejudice in this case. This person's kind of activity apparently had no precedent in the body's experience. It was not "central," that is, literary in a familiar mode. This fate frequently befalls people who work in subjects like teaching English in the secondary schools and perform liaison with the secondary schools. Publication here seems to be the stumbling block. No one asks whether publication is the most desirable form of activity for such people. Possibly less important standards would not be applied as strongly if we took such activities more seriously and had more people in the department doing much-needed liaison work.

Not too long ago creative writers, so-called, were in a similar fix; and before that the American literature teachers. In my own field of literary theory and criticism, one hears cases of what can only charitably be called neglect of (malice against is a better phrase) such practitioners, and this has led to the playing out of revenge plots of such crude simplicity that no one other than a genius like Shakespeare would have considered them useful. What a waste this is.

A monolithic notion of English breeds dissension and paranoia. There will always be competition among the disciplines of English and not enough spoils to satisfy anyone. But there are interrelations, too, and interdependences of subtle kinds. Department chairs should support the interdependences. Some things will always seem more important at one time, some at another. Some disciplines may disappear or change drastically. What is important is a sense of interrelation and mutual respect. The usual strategies of self-protection militate against interrelationship and mutual respect.

Certainly large departments like English must accept a good share of blame for the abominable state of general, or as I would prefer to call it, were it better, liberal education in the universities and colleges. The wrong strategy is for a large department to try to protect itself by refusing to give up anything, no matter how trivial, for the sake of a larger enterprise. Overwhelming size ought to allow room for some magnanimity. From the point of view of many departments English is overwhelming. English ought to lead in bringing some intellectual principle into what is usually called a smorgasbord but is more like my memory of the chow line at Parris Island, where the milk tasted of garlic, the eggs were powdered, and breakfast was consistently served at the wrong hour. English must lead because no smaller department has the strength to, though many can contribute out of proportion to their size, to their advantage, if given help. A strong program in general liberal education is the best protection against suicide that I know— for large or small departments in the humanities.

At least, an alternative to the commonly used distribution lists of courses should be developed. My choice would be a program of courses that would probe beneath what usually goes on in introductory courses in a discipline. I would like to see a package of courses of four types: First, courses that inquire into the grounds, whether philosophical or practical, for proceeding as one conventionally does in a certain discipline. This would involve reflecting critically and analytically on the assumptions generally made, their limits, and their potentialities. Second, courses that inquire into the relations between a discipline and the culture at large, including the academic culture and, in some cases, the local community. Third, courses that inquire into questions posed and approached in different ways by different disciplines and that study the implications of the differences and possible meeting points. Fourth, courses that study the history of disciplines.

In recent years, quite a few courses have been developed that do one or more of these things. Frequently they have been developed by professors who have come into touch with linguistic, anthropological, and/or literary theory; or they have been concerned with the social implications of scientific developments. This phenomenon has many sources in the culture and ought to be studied in itself. One of them surely is that the proliferation of disciplines has quite naturally set in motion an urgent questioning even of what questions ought to be or can be asked. Do the old definitions of human being suffice? What possible new ones are emerging and what do they forebode? Some people may say that these questions belong only to philosophy or to anthropology. But I believe that the questioning going on now belongs to us all and that a discipline that does not arrange to ask them risks being justly perceived as trivial.

I am reminded here of Nietzsche's recounting the argument of Schopenhauer in his acerbic *On University Philosophy:* "Non-academical men have good grounds for a certain general contempt of the universities; they say reproachfully that they are cowardly, that the small ones are afraid of the large ones, and that the large ones are afraid of public opinion; that in none of the questions of higher culture do the universities take the lead, but always limp slow and late in the rear." Moreover, there is much alarm if anyone succeeds in advancing to the front. Recently in the *Times Literary Supplement* (10 Dec. 1982) an interesting symposium on the subject of "professing literature" included statements by Paul de Man, E. D. Hirsch, Jr., René Wellek, Raymond Williams, and Stanley Fish, among others. It evoked a certain amount of correspondence, the most violent of which was two letters by Donald Reiman (7 Jan. and 18 Feb. 1983), the well-known scholar of romanticism, who vented his spleen against those he characterizes as "mountebanks," mainly from Yale, and specifically Paul de Man and Jacques Derrida. They have, in their disciplines, insisted on asking difficult, even embarrassing questions and questioning the asking. Reiman's claim seemed to be that these people are destroying all morality and making literary study into an elitist occupation concerned not with the "egalitarian tradition" but instead with "issues of philosophy, psychology, and rhetoric" as they define these things. This is an old cry, and it has almost always been wrongheaded and never, as far as I know, success-

ful in stemming the tide. It has been heard about everyone
who has ever come along and challenged us to think. Reiman's
way of protecting the profession is but an exaggeration of the
drawing in that plagues departments in moments of intellectual opportunity. It sets people against people in unproductive
ways and frustrates reasoned argument. If you suspect that
something is wrong with Paul de Man's argument, study it and
join in the debate. It is an opportunity to think. Reiman feels
that to do this would take him away from his "real work,"
which, apparently fixed and sanctified in his mind, is in no
way to be questioned, while de Man's, he implies, is not only
trivial but also evil. It is sad to see Walter Jackson Bate in a
recent issue of the *Harvard Magazine* performing in an equally
anti-intellectual way against the same targets.

Another unfortunate form of self-protection involves refusal
to accept new forms of intellectual life that could very well
become a part of English studies. We have retrieved and taught
many not very good old plays (as well as some terrible new
ones) on grounds of historical importance, but we have been
loath, for example, to treat the filming of the better old plays.
There is no reason not to have an English course on the filming
of Shakespeare. (There are such courses in some places now.)
The course need not address all the known questions surrounding film, but it could well formulate literary and linguistic issues and consider the relation of a performance to a
text. Certainly the adaptation of novels to film is another area
of interesting critical activity. In time, of course, there will be a
considerable literature of television drama that will demand
address as well. These are but simple and obvious examples.

Recent theorizing has raised important questions about the
boundaries of literature and even the term "literature" itself.
Some of us have viewed this questioning with alarm. On the
whole it has been a good thing. No one had ever said that English was an exclusively literary discipline until about 1938,
and then it was with the motive of pressing for the study of

certain kinds of texts in a roughly contextualist fashion, not to
make English departments devoted exclusively to them. We
now are more able to recognize the significance of many sorts
of works that were relegated to the periphery: autobiography,
biography, some philosophical and historical writing, and even
scientific texts. This ought to mean that we have more to say to
other disciplines than we have been used to thinking, that we
have a larger role to play in liberal education than we have been
playing. That role jibes with the program I have suggested for
a new liberal education requirement.

Finally, under my second principle, it seems to me that English departments attempt suicide when they are either self-
protectively closed or aggressively colonialistic. There are
many subjects taught narrowly in English departments that
would be better taught in cooperation with other departments,
were there a genuine spirit of intellectual give-and-take among
those naturally involved. In each of my three fields—the history of criticism and theory, English romanticism, and modern
Anglo-Irish literature—I can imagine different forms of cooperation. The first surely ought to be taught interdependently,
probably by a team involving classicists, Germanicists, Slavi-
cists, professors of French, of Italian, and of English. The history of criticism and theory is an international subject. To escape the parochial, English departments ought to take the lead
in expanding the enterprise. English romanticism has its own
character, different from French or German, or so Lovejoy insisted. Whether he was right or not, a course in English romanticism must refer to German philosophy and French history, at the least, and it would make sense to develop some
cooperative ventures with other departments. Modern Anglo-
Irish literature is deeply embedded in little-known Irish history, where a historian would be a big help. As a large department English ought to foster the intellectual relations that
smaller departments are less likely, through fear, to seek. I believe that in large institutions the first step in such a program is

to collect people from various departments in colloquiums on such subjects, for interrelations always have to begin with people of goodwill and common interests. In this way many of the tensions that now exist between academic units in their abstract suspicions of each other might be alleviated. No, changed to become productive rather than negative tensions. To bring off these kinds of relations is a long-range project. Many who advocate and set forth on such efforts do not grasp how different the traditions, intellectual styles, and even personality types of the various disciplines are. The aim ought to be not to level these styles but to come to understand them as vehicles for seeing things from different perspectives; but also some leveling would not hurt.

The nice thing about my last two principles is that since they follow from the first and second ones my remarks can be brief. Principle the Third: *Too much order creates disorder.* Heraclitus said about the universe what should be said about English departments: Homer was wrong, one of his surviving fragments reads, to pray for the end of strife, because that would be to pray for the end of the universe. Still, some forms of strife are preferable to others and some are definitely pernicious. Blake knew this in his distinction between contraries and negations. In a negation, one side of an opposition achieves an unwholesome domination. In a contrary, strife exists for the sake of friendship. For the most part, in history negations rule in cyclical alternation. Whether Blake would have called deconstruction an example of the negating "idiot questioner" of his prophetic books I do not know. He was a bit of a deconstructor himself, and I think he would have thought in some cases its skepticism against blind faith in past methods a little tame and possessed of not enough indignation. The leading deconstructionist advocates examination of all one's premises and the questioning of the idea of a premise as well as the questioning of the question. Followers have quickly made a dogma here, and that is a Blakean negation. This means we must be skeptical of skepticism as faith. This is the best form of disorder I know. In the "professing literature" symposium Raymond Williams calls for diversity. He likes the idea of recognizable academic styles issuing from different places. English departments in American institutions are so large that such a notion would, if possible to be put into practice, create a series of huge monoliths, the main function of which would be the terrorizing of the most imaginative assistant professors. Large departments should themselves contain diversity. Probably at any given time some aspects of a department's activity will be most popular, be perceived (probably wrongly) as expressing its entire character, as has been true at times at Chicago, Yale, and Irvine. This will seem threatening to some people. What is most important here is that those who are at the moment popular recognize the worth of other activities and take pains to emphasize their importance. Students are susceptible to fashion, and the leaders of it should recognize transience and endlessly advocate the restoration of disorder.

Principle the Fourth: *Disciplinary purity breeds self-destruction.* As certain breeds of dog have become more beautiful, delicate, and softer of fur, so have they begun to lose eyesight, suffer dislocation of the hip, and become subject to various other genetic diseases. As classics departments at one time nearly disappeared, from refusing to exploit the relation of their literatures to modern literatures and of their methods to the methods of modern criticism, so it could be with larger departments that seek to purify their subjects. Much of the negative response to "professing literature" in the *TLS* involved a fear that literary study was once again being perceived in foreign, mainly effete French, ways and that these ways were being taught to unsuspecting northeasterners by dangerous and insidious professors, all at Yale or trained there. G. S. Rousseau in his letter (28 Jan. 1983) trying to straighten out some of Donald Reiman's excesses and errors of historical interpretation—though, I think, sympathetic to Reiman's general fear—put his finger on the major question. Reiman, he said, "never acknowledges that the same development [the fashionableness of theory] is occurring in *other* fields as well: history, the social sciences, the natural sciences." This is, of course, quite true; and it marks a major intellectual change that English departments might see as an opportunity in ways I have implied. The consequences of rigid opposition will be, I fear, far more severe and far-reaching than opposition to any shift of past critical fashion has produced. Either English departments will have to assimilate this new questioning movement to their activities, or the kind of questioning that has been unleashed will begin to destroy the present organization of academic disciplines as we know them, taking with it, no doubt, any notion of literature or criticism in the traditional sense. Assimilation and flexibility here mean welcoming questions, accepting them in the curriculum, and questioning them. By and large the most popular new movements are social-scientific and ahistorical or, when historical, strongly antihumanistic. Yet my view, in the face of what some see only as a threat, is that the humanistic can always, with the proper ingenuity, contain such movements and that such movements cannot finally satisfactorily contain the humanistic. They never know quite what to do about it; unless the humanists close in on themselves and play dead.

In the process of assimilation, it must be remembered that students tend to fly to fashion, knowing little else, and that when departments recruit faculty in order to contain a dominant fashion they risk acquiring in a decade or so an accumulation of deadwood. The signs of New Critical deadwood have been around us for some time. Soon, the lesser deconstructionists and lesser feminists will pile up in the lumber room with them. Unlike professional sports, our profession cannot often give an unconditional release.

In my own view, the study of the history of one's subject is the best antidote to slavery to fashion. For many of us, it may be the history of criticism, for others the history of linguistics or the teaching of English, and so forth. Merely to name these histories is to see that they are interrelated and that study of one generates interest in the others. Here we find relation in difference, unless, of course, one subscribes to the popular notion that history is bunk. There we find ourselves in one of the true contraries of our time, worth a debate that would raise issues I have been speaking of in a most compelling way. Is the view that history is bunk a ground to abandon history, or is it, itself, to be perceived as a historical phenomenon? Heraclitus would have enjoyed this strife, which appears to me to be the antinomy that follows on my principles.

To resist strife in the name of purity is a philosophical mistake. It is also a tactical one in the profession of teaching. It leaves one's students unable to cope with new languages and cuts them off from fruitful debate. New languages are often offensive, new writers frequently unnecessarily obscure and full of jargon. Someone else's critical jargon is the first refuge of innocence and the eternal home of followers. Many innocents are writing theory or about theory today or applying theoretical languages where they think it will do some good (i.e., give them tenure). But there has always been innocence written large in every discipline: in all fields of English, not just theory. And there will be, as long as universities tell young faculty to write and to write in innocence (i.e., in a hurry). At the same time, I can't think of too many writers who didn't raise the hackles of their readers at first. Most contemporary theoretical writing, I must admit, irritates me. I wish they would all write like Hume and call a spade a spade like Johnson. I admit to lingering resentment of Hegel. But I'd be a fool if I suggested to students that Hegel be avoided or declared a "mountebank." I am willing to try to discover with my students where Paul de Man goes wrong, if he does, but only after I address his argument with respect and in the process acknowledge that I know my own better for having addressed it.

And now I have finished, my principles set forth. Whether they are worth further examination is for you to decide.

DEFINITION
AND/AS SURVIVAL

WHENEVER THERE IS declared to be a crisis in literary study—
that is, a putative diminishment of enrollments in English—I
am reminded of two things. The first is that this country is
very large and that generalizations made to include all of it
seem always a little provincial. Not too long ago I read an essay
by George Rousseau deploring that undergraduates are no
longer studying eighteenth-century English literature. It was a
gloom-and-doom essay of considerable eloquence. But recently the associate chair of my department expressed concern
that we are turning away undergraduates from eighteenth-
century courses and need to offer more classes in the field. The
second thing I am reminded of is a remark made to me decades
ago by a professor, a veteran of the red-baiting years in Seattle,
circa 1948–52: "If the public *really* knew what we *really* do,
then you'd *really* see trouble."

I could go on and add another remembrance or two along
these lines: For example, thirty-five years or more ago discour-
agement fell not on teachers of the eighteenth century but on
those of romanticism, under pressure from new critical taste,
who deplored the failure of a generation to appreciate Shelley,
Byron, and the simple Wordsworth. It took the ingenious
efforts of Northrop Frye, once a few people understood what

179

he had been getting at in *Fearful Symmetry*, and then a trickle of books by a new generation of critics, inspired partly by him and partly by a confluence of other ideas, to change the situation radically. Things got so bad in the sixties that in order to protect myself against the hordes who intended to breathe in an ectoplasm they called William Blake, I was forced to announce on the first day of class that Blake was after all merely an eighteenth-century rationalist, though he thought otherwise, and that I intended to teach him as such. This simple statement partially emptied the classroom of those who, I mean man, were not going to accept any professional interference with a Blake turn-on or tune-out.

I note that I have inadvertently hit on my theme of definition and/as survival, though I had not intended to begin with this somewhat personal and idiosyncratic example. My remembrances are meant to suggest that because of the academy's tendency to inertia things have seldom been either as bad or as good as they seemed. Or, to read the other side of this coin, there is always a crisis. Still, every generation of academics or every era faces new problems, which evoke anxieties in specific places, attack specific nerves, and sometimes seem to bode apocalypse.

Perhaps the nerve most susceptible among academic humanists is the one touched when periodically we need to defend ourselves by definition or, to put it more accurately, to describe our role in academic society to some supposedly alien body. Our impulses—and I think they are natural ones, based on an accurate tacit assessment of what we do and stand for and what our inquisitors grasp of all this—are to give some less straightforward version of Louis Armstrong's nonexplanation of jazz, to retire with momentary appearance of dignity behind a few cant phrases, or to refuse to play on the ground that proper answers can't be given except at book length and that, in fact, we are writing on that very subject at this very time, please have patience. None of these tactics has ever helped at all with a state legislator or with an academic administration composed mainly of behavioral scientists charmed by notions of competence tests. It is true that high-sounding phrases can, if kept reasonably up to date, appeal for a while to administrators late of the pure and elite sciences. The moral here is probably that one must regard these sorts of definitions as weapons in the more elevated ritual skirmishes of academic politics, best invented and uttered by what I shall call the true poets among chairpeople, whom if a department has any sense it will elect as leaders to embellish the myths of the tribe when the verbal coin has been rubbed smooth and when there is occasion for ritual defense.

What is really important is definition to oneself, the decisions a department makes, sometimes silently, within itself. Internal definition is important because, first, most externalized definitions are merely part of some mysterious ongoing process, like the infamous, constantly updated five-year plan or copy for the university catalog. Here the terms of my title, "definition" and "survival," can well be separated by "and." Second, such externalized definitions will have important effects and will actually mean something only if some internal decision has caused the departmental spokespersons to utter real thoughts. The internal process of definition *is* survival. I hold that periods of silent definition are inferior to those of open debate, that we err, in the present circumstances and perhaps in all circumstances (since all situations have uniqueness), in not seeking self-definition openly and even deliberately by painful internal discussion. The trouble is that the hardest questions come first: What are the facts? Here are two as I see them. They are perhaps as challengeable as George Rousseau's remarks about eighteenth-century studies. Still, I offer them:

(1) Given the traditional aims of graduate study, as the inertia of English departments tends silently to define them, there are too many graduate students and graduate programs. It is possible that many English departments themselves know

this, are genuinely pained by it, and would either sharply de- crease the size of their programs or change their aim if both options did not seem, with good reason, formulas for suicide. Why? Because the university rewards departments for having a large proportion of graduate students, often encouraging a department to enlarge and simultaneously castigating the same department for not putting enough resources into lower- division teaching. At the same time the teaching budget is funded in such a way as to force the department (usually at the last minute) to employ low-paid helots, namely graduate stu- dent teachers, to do its work, thus requiring large graduate student populations. This steady state I shall call the unher- meneuted circle, because everyone turns to it a deaf ear. That is, no one responds to it. If it were heard and acted against, the result would be revolutionary. To tell the story of this circle in the corridors of academic power is to hear the doors shut up and down those halls. It is a story no one wants to hear, because it challenges fundamental institutional patterns of behavior.

If, given the present astonishing oversupply of potential col- lege teachers, the traditional definitions remain, most places are bound to have problems. In order to deal with them certain institutions would have to acknowledge and act against my unhermeneuted circle. This will not happen even by depart- mental choice, because in the short term no one would like it. Many prospective graduate students would be turned away, more faculty members would teach more lower-division courses, and so on. If by some miracle it did happen and mo- rale were salvaged, perhaps undergraduate education would improve. After a few years maybe the department's best minds would pay more attention to undergraduate study. Don't bet on any of it happening. Rather more likely is an elaboration of a recent piety—that graduate study is really for those who wish to fulfill independent, personal intellectual goals, to expand their horizons, to activate their potential, especially for those who at a more advanced age have the leisure to read, think, and study. This is a convenient fiction at best. It is not in the nature of things, but if it were and if departments took it seriously, it would necessitate a wholesale rethinking of graduate programs, including curricula and teaching methods. It won't happen.

(2) Given the realities, not this pleasant romantic fiction of thirst for human knowledge among those with leisure—knowledge to be consumed according to traditional graduate school rites—the present-day graduate student is plagued by a stupendous burgeoning of apparently contending forces. I shall not recite them except to remark that the uncertainties of the job market, intensified competition, the plethora of publication in all subjects, and the broadening of the intellectual field make hitherto unheard-of demands. Unless departments can work up some new order out of this teeming mass—an order that is not devastatingly reductive—students and faculty alike will retire to narrow specializations at the very intellectual moment when specializing in anything has come to require a special sort of breadth. (You will note that I do not decry specialization. It is absolutely necessary to contemporary life, but it must be redefined.)

We have been witnessing in this century a radical revision of what lies beneath any special knowledge, a radical change in what one must know or, let us say, consider or question to accomplish any one intellectual task. Probably we are as yet at the beginning of this change, which is not merely technological and embodied in the computer—or, for the English professor, the word processor—but is reshaping our sense of intellectual need in myriad ways. This is why in our disciplines literary theory has had such rapid development as a major, ubiquitous force and why there are so many disagreements in theory, many of which at this stage are really logical independences. This condition is not a fad likely to go the way of disco dancing; it is present today in virtually every field, and it expresses an effort to cope with new, startling developments. So many received truths have been so tellingly questioned that all disciplines look to their grounds, which seem sometimes a chaos or an abyss. Our national political situation may be the last ineffective refusal of an inevitable adventure.

It is clear that we will have to put advanced literary study together in a new way; and, as must be usual in such situations, we are not well equipped by habit to do so, let alone to imagine a new shape. All intelligent graduate students must be aware of this dilemma, and we may have to learn what to do about graduate study in part from observing how the best of them are working around our anachronisms and managing to educate themselves for what they imagine their needs will be. In any case, graduate programs will have to be more efficient because the mass of things to know about is not only immeasurably greater but more complex and varied.

I came here not to attempt answers but to set some questions. Still, I offer three things that I think ought to be accomplished:

(1) We must make the study of foreign languages more important to English PhD's. We can no longer pay lip service to this requirement and expect our graduates to do significant work. The linguistic incapacity of American PhD's has always been a joke; in the present intellectual situation it has become a scandal. Obviously adjustments must be made in the present curriculum to rescue this situation. Teachers would have to urge their students to know foreign languages better. Don't bet that they will, though surely they ought to, if only as part of a general effort to make more Americans capable of using a foreign language. This effort must be pressed in undergraduate, secondary, and primary education.

(2) We must better understand the history of literary theory, by which I mean we must be capable of writing and rewriting it. As in all subjects today the rewriters will have to pay attention to things never remarked by previous historians of this subject. In this enterprise, we shall better discover what we

should be doing and teaching; thus we shall be reformulating the structure of the discipline. This agendum speaks to a need already mentioned: just as potential bibliographical scholars are faced with a revolution in their methods that requires familiarity with areas not known to many of us, so in theory, which these days is so protean, we must take seriously the need to learn from other arts and sciences.

(3) There must be intense study of the history of academic disciplines. Luckily such work has begun. There are at least two reasons for this imperative. One is that our debilitating communal anxiety about change is often traceable to our ignorance of past change and a frequently unwarranted belief that our present ways are sanctified not only by common sense but also by long tradition. Another is that we and our students lack sufficient survival gear, one important item of which is an understanding of our profession and of the politics of academic life; thus as humanists we are far less effective than we could be in pursuing our institutional ends, whatever they may be. Instead of taking the competency or behavioral-science approach to this matter, which schools of education have already shown to be inadequate, I recommend the more indirect approach of historical understanding to make us better academic politicians. In today's intellectual chaos—which I suspect will turn out to be a second renaissance, if we do not blow ourselves up—we in English must begin to produce not only a few academic Machiavellis but also their active students, because as history tells us, in a renaissance power devolves on the strong, the intelligent, and the learned and on those, I would add, who can articulate a definition of their worth, at least to themselves and maybe even to those quite shrewd legislators from Dime Box, Opportunity, Wagon Tire, and American Fork.